Books on Egypt and Chaldaea

THE EGYPTIAN HEAVEN AND HELL

BY

E. A. WALLIS BUDGE, M.A., LITT.D., D.LITT., D.LIT.

KEEPER OF THE EGYPTIAN AND ASSYRIAN ANTIQUITIES
IN THE BRITISH MUSEUM

VOL. III.

THE CONTENTS OF THE BOOKS OF THE OTHER WORLD DESCRIBED AND COMPARED

ISBN: 978-1-63182-833-1

Printed: March 2023

Published and Distributed By:
Lushena Books
607 Country Club Drive, Unit E
Bensenville, IL 60106
www.lushenabks.com

ISBN: 978-1-63182-833-1

cene from the Papyrus of Nekht, showing the deceased and his wife worshipping Osiris in the Other World, and the manner of the house in which they expected to live, and their vineyard and garden with its lake of water. (British Museum, No. 10,471, sheet 21.)

PREFACE

THE present work is the outcome of two lectures on the Books of the Ṭuat, i.e., the Egyptian Underworld, or "Other World," which I had the honour to deliver at the Royal Institution in the spring of 1904, and it has been prepared at the suggestion of many who wished to continue their inquiries into the beliefs of the Egyptians concerning the abode of the departed, and the state of the blessed and the damned.

The object of all the Books of the Other World was to provide the dead with a "Guide" or "Handbook," which contained a description of the regions through which their souls would have to pass on their way to the kingdom of Osiris, or to that portion of the sky where the sun rose, and which would supply them with the words of power and magical names necessary for making an unimpeded journey from this world to the abode of the blessed. For a period of two thousand years in the history of Egypt, the Books of the Other World consisted of texts only, but about B.C. 2500 funeral artists began to represent pictorially the chief features of the "Field of Peace," or "Islands of the Blessed," and before the close of the XIXth Dynasty, about 1300 years later, all the principal books relating to the Ṭuat were profusely illustrated. In the copies of them which were painted on the walls of royal tombs, each division of the Ṭuat was clearly drawn and described, and each gate, with all its guardians, was carefully depicted. Both the living and the dead could learn from them, not only the names, but also the forms, of every god, spirit, soul, shade, demon, and monster which they were likely to meet on their way, and the copious texts which were given side by side with the pictures enabled the traveller through the Ṭuat—always, of course, provided that he had learned them—to participate in the benefits which were decreed by the Sun-god for the beings of each section of it.

In primitive times each great city of Egypt possessed its own Other World, and, no doubt, the priests of each city provided the worshippers of their gods with suitable "guides" to the abode of its dead. In the beginning of the Dynastic Period, however, we find that the cult of Osiris was extremely popular, and therefore it was only natural that great numbers of people in all parts of Egypt should hope and believe that their souls after death would go to the kingdom in the Other World over which he reigned. The beliefs connected with the cult of Osiris developed naturally out of the beliefs of the Predynastic Egyptians, who, we have every reason to think, dealt largely in magic both "Black" and "White." Many of the superstitions, and most of the fantastic and half-savage ideas about the gods and supernatural powers enshrined in the great collection of religious texts called PER-EM-HRU, were inherited by the Dynastic Egyptians from some of the oldest dwellers in the Nile Valley. Those who died in the faith of Osiris believed in the efficacy of the Book PER-EM-HRU, and were content to employ it as a "Guide" to a heaven which was full of material delights; the number of those who were "followers" of Osiris was very large under every dynasty in Egypt. On the other hand, from the IVth Dynasty onwards there was a very large class who had no belief in a purely material heaven, and this being so, it is not surprising that Books of the Other World containing the expression of their views should be composed.

The principal Books of the Underworld in vogue under the XVIIIth and XIXth Dynasties were:— 1. PER-EM-HRU, or, "[The Book] of the Coming Forth by Day." 2. SHĀT ENT ÅM ṬUAT, or, "The Book of that which is in the Ṭuat." 3. The composition to which the name "Book of Gates" has been given. Now the first of these, which is commonly known as the "Theban Recension of the Book of the Dead," has supplied us with much valuable information about the beliefs which flourished in connection with an early form of the ancient cult of Osiris in the Delta, and with the later form of his worship, after he had absorbed the position and attributes of Khenti-Ȧmenti, an old local deity of Abydos. The two other Books, however, are as important, each in its own way, as the "Book of the Dead," for they throw considerable light on the development of the material and spiritual elements in the religion of Egypt, and commemorate the belief in the existence of numbers of primitive gods, who are unknown outside these Books. The "Book Ȧm-Ṭuat," in the form in which we know it, was drawn up by the priests of the confraternity of Ȧmen-Rā at Thebes, with the express object of demonstrating that their god was the overlord of all the gods, and the supreme power in "Pet Ta Ṭuat," or, as we should say, "Heaven, Earth, and Hell." The Ṭuat, or Other World, which they imagined included the Ṭuat of every great district of Egypt, viz., the Ṭuat of Khenti-Ȧmenti at Abydos, the Ṭuat of Seker of Memphis, the Ṭuat of Osiris of Mendes, and the Ṭuat of Temu-Kheper-Rā of Heliopolis.

In the BOOḲ ȦM-ṬUAT the god Ȧmen-Rā was made to pass through all these Ṭuats as their overlord and god, and his priests taught that all the gods of the dead, including Osiris, lived through his words, and that such refreshing as the beings of the Ṭuat enjoyed each day was due to his grace and light during his passage through their regions and Circles. Moreover, according to the dogmas of the priests of Ȧmen-Rā, only those who were fortunate enough to secure a place in the divine bark of the god could hope to traverse the Ṭuat unharmed, and only those who were his elect had the certainty of being re-born daily, with a new supply of strength and life, and of becoming of like nature and substance with him.

In the Book of Gates the dogmas and doctrines of Osiris are far more prominent, and the state of the beatified closely resembles that described in the "Book of the Dead." In primitive times in Egypt men thought that they would obtain admission into the kingdom of Ḥetep by learning and remembering the secret name of this god and certain magical formulae, and by pronouncing them in the correct way at the proper time. The need for a consciousness of sin, and repentance, and a life of good works, were not then held to be indispensable for admission into the abode of the beatified. From the "Book of Gates," however, we learn that in the later Dynastic Period a belief was prevalent that those who worshipped the "great god" on earth, and made all the duly-appointed offerings, and turned not aside to "miserable little gods," and lived according to *maāt*, i.e., uprightness and integrity, would receive a good reward *because* they had done these things. The texts in these Books state that the beatified live for ever in the kingdom of Osiris, and feed daily upon the heavenly wheat of righteousness that springs from the body of Osiris, which is eternal; he is righteousness itself, and they are righteous, and they live by eating the body of their god daily. On the other hand, the wicked, i.e., those who did not believe in the great god or make offerings, are hacked to pieces by the divine messengers of wrath, and their bodies, souls, and spirits are consumed by fire once and for all.

The Egyptians had no belief in a purgatory. The fires of the Other World were, it is true, occupied daily in burning up the damned and the opponents of the Sun-god, but each day brought its own supply of bodies, souls, spirits, demons, etc., for annihilation. In all the Books of the Other World we find pits of fire, abysses of darkness, murderous knives, streams of boiling water, foul stenches, fiery serpents, hideous animal-headed monsters and creatures, and cruel, death-dealing beings of various shapes, etc., similar to those with which we are familiar in early Christian and mediæval literature, and it is tolerably certain that modern nations are indebted to Egypt for many of their conceptions of hell.

In the present work the object has been to give the reader the complete hieroglyphic texts of the BOOK ȦM-ṬUAT and the BOOK OF GATES, with reproductions of all their illustrations in black and white, and English translations and descriptions. The illustrations of the former work have been specially traced from the plates of the excellent edition of the tomb of Seti I. published by MM. G. Lefébure, U. Bouriant, V. Loret, and E. Naville, in the second volume of the *Mémoires de la Mission Archéologique Française au Caire*, Paris, 1886. The illustrations of the BOOK OF GATES have been traced from Bonomi's *Sarcophagus of Oimenepthah I.*, London, 1864, but for certain scenes I was permitted by the late Mr. G. Birch, Keeper of Sir John Soane's Museum, to compare the tracings with the scenes on the sarcophagus itself. A copy of the scene on the portion of the cover, which I acquired for the Trustees of the British Museum a few years ago, has also been included.

The plan followed has been to devote a chapter to each Division of the Ṭuat, and to give the hieroglyphic texts, with short descriptions of the various gods, &c., and translations, as near to the scenes to which they refer as possible. With a view of making the edition as complete as possible, I have added a transcript of the "Summary" of the Book Åm-Ṭuat from Dr. Pleyte's facsimile of the Leyden Papyrus, and a translation for the convenience of the reader who may wish to compare the Divisions of Åm-Ṭuat with those of the Book of Gates. The former have been printed in one volume, and the latter in another; the full index given at the end of the introductory volume will, it is hoped, make reference and comparison easy. All general descriptions, and such explanations of the scenes as are possible in the present state of our knowledge, have been given in a series of chapters in this volume, together with an account of the origin and development of "guides" to the Other World, and a rendering of a recently published and very important text from a coffin at Cairo. This text proves that the

Egyptians believed in the reconstitution of family life in the Other World, and thought that every man, and woman, and child would possess such a measure of individuality that they would know their relatives and friends in the Other World, and would be known by them (see within, Chapter III.).

The first translation of the BOOK ÅM-ṬUAT was published by Prof. G. Maspero in the *Revue des Religions*, 1888, tom. xvii., pp. 251—310; tom. xviii., pp. 1—67. This has been reprinted, with certain modifications and additions, in his *Bibliothèque Égyptologique*, tom. ii., pp. 1—181, Paris, 1893. The text chosen by him for elucidation was that published by M. G. Lefébure in his edition of the tomb of Seti I., and this he supplemented with extracts from other versions of the work given on sarcophagi, papyri, etc. The "Summary," or Short Form of ÅM-ṬUAT, was first published in a complete form, with variant readings, by M. G. Jéquier (see his *Le Ḷivre de ce qu'il y a dans l'Hades*, Paris, 1894). In Prof. Maspero's work mentioned above he also discussed and analysed the earlier sections of the BOOK OF GATES, of which M. E. Lefébure published a translation of the texts, as found on the sarcophagus of Seti I., in the *Records of the Past*, vol. x., pp. 79—134, London, 1878, and vol. xii., pp. 1—35, London, 1881. In preparing the present edition of the two great Books of the Other World I have availed myself of these works, and also of the valuable editions of the texts from the royal tombs at Thebes, which M. E. Lefébure has published in the first and second fasciculi of the third volume of the *Mémoires de la Mission Archéologique Française au Caire*, Paris, 1889.

E. A. WALLIS BUDGE.

LONDON,
October, 1905.

CONTENTS

CHAP.		PAGE
I.	ORIGIN OF ILLUSTRATED GUIDES TO THE OTHER WORLD	1
II.	THE EARLIEST EGYPTIAN CONCEPTION OF THE OTHER WORLD	27
III.	THE REUNION OF THE BEATIFIED AND THEIR RECOGNITION OF EACH OTHER IN THE OTHER WORLD	64
	APPENDIX:—THE CHAPTER OF THE GATHERING TOGETHER OF A MAN'S ANCESTORS TO HIM IN NETER-KHER	75
IV.	THE BOOK ÀM-ṬUAT AND THE BOOK OF GATES	80
V.	THE BOOK ÀM-ṬUAT AND THE BOOK OF GATES COMPARED—THE WESTERN VESTIBULE OF THE ṬUAT	103
VI.	SECOND DIVISION OF THE ṬUAT	111
VII.	THIRD DIVISION OF THE ṬUAT	121
VIII.	FOURTH AND FIFTH DIVISIONS OF THE ṬUAT. FROM THE BOOK ÀM-ṬUAT	131
IX.	FOURTH AND FIFTH DIVISIONS OF THE ṬUAT. FROM THE BOOK OF GATES	140
X.	SIXTH, SEVENTH, EIGHTH, AND NINTH DIVISIONS OF THE ṬUAT. FROM THE BOOK ÀM-ṬUAT	148

CHAP.		PAGE
XI.	Sixth, Seventh, and Eighth Divisions of the Ṭuat. From the Book of Gates . . .	158
XII.	Tenth and Eleventh Divisions of the Ṭuat. From the Book Ám-Ṭuat	172
XIII.	Ninth, Tenth, and Eleventh Divisions of the Ṭuat. From the Book of Gates . . .	182
XIV.	The Eastern Vestibule of the Ṭuat . .	192

LIST OF ILLUSTRATIONS.

	PAGE
Scene from the Papyrus of Nekht . .	*Frontispiece*
The Seven Ārits and their Warders	29
The Ten Gates and their Warders . . .	32-35
The Fourteen Åats	38-41
Sekhet-ḥetep. From the Papyrus of Nebseni . .	43
" " " " Ani . . .	45
" Ḳua-tep . .	54
" Coffin of Sen . . .	55
" " " Papyrus of Ånhai . .	60
" " " " Ptolemaïc Period	61
Nekht spearing the Eater of the Ass	113
The Boat of the Earth	126
The Serpent Āsht-ḥråu	149
Nebseni being weighed against his Heart . . .	159
The Scales of Osiris, with weights	159
The Judgment Hall of Osiris	161
Nekht spearing the Pig of Evil	163
The Apes working the Net	184

THE
EGYPTIAN HEAVEN AND HELL

CHAPTER I.

ORIGIN OF ILLUSTRATED GUIDES TO THE OTHER WORLD.

THE inhabitants of Egypt during the Dynastic Period of their history possessed, in common with other peoples of similar antiquity, very definite ideas about the abode of departed spirits, but few, if any, ancient nations caused their beliefs about the situation and form, and divisions, and inhabitants of their Heaven and Hell, or "Other World," to be described so fully in writing, and none have illustrated the written descriptions of their beliefs so copiously with pictorial representations of the gods and devils, and the good and evil spirits and other beings, who were supposed to exist in the kingdom of the dead. It is now generally admitted that Egyptian Dynastic History covers a period of nearly five thousand years, but it must not be assumed for one moment that it is at present possible to describe in a connected or complete form all the views and opinions about their Other World which were held by the theologians and the uneducated classes of Egypt during this long space of time, and it must be said at once that the materials for such a work are not forthcoming. All that can be done is to collect from the copies that have come down to us of the books which relate to the state and condition of the dead, and to the abode of departed spirits, the beliefs which are enunciated or referred to therein, and, taking them so far as possible in chronological order, to piece them together and then make deductions and draw general conclusions from them. We must always remember that the texts of the various Books of the Dead are far older than the illustrations found in the later recensions of them which are now in our hands, and that such illustrations, in matters of detail at least, reflect the opinions of the priestly class that held religious supremacy at the time when they were drawn or painted. In cases where archetypes were available the artist was careful to follow in all general matters the ancient copies to which he had access, but when new beliefs and new religious conceptions had to be illustrated, he was free to treat them pictorially according to his own knowledge, and according to the wishes of those who employed him.

The oldest Books of the Dead known to us, that is to say, the religious compositions which are inscribed on the walls of the chambers and corridors of the pyramids of kings Unȧs, Tetȧ, Pepi I., Mer-en-Rā, and Pepi II., are without illustrations of any sort or kind, and it is not easy to account for this fact. That the Egyptians possessed artistic skill sufficient to illustrate the religious and general works which their theologians wrote or revised, under their earliest dynasties of kings of all Egypt, is evident from the plain and coloured bas-reliefs which adorn the walls of their *maṣṭabas*, or bench-shaped tombs, and we can only point out and wonder at the fact that the royal pyramids contain neither painted nor sculptured vignettes, especially as pictures are much needed to break the monotony of the hundreds of lines of large hieroglyphics, painted in a bluish-green colour, which must have dazzled the eyes even of an Egyptian. The reason, however, why such early texts are not illustrated is probably not far to seek. Professor Maspero has proved that the "pyramid texts" contain formulae and paragraphs which, judging from the grammatical forms that occur in them, it is easy to see must have been composed, if not actually written down, in the earliest times of Egyptian civilization. These formulae, &c., are interspersed with others of later periods, and it seems as if, at the time when the "pyramid texts" were cut into stone, these religious compositions were intended to contain expressions of pious thought about the hereafter which would satisfy both those who accepted the ancient indigenous beliefs, and those who were prepared to believe the doctrines which had been promulgated by the priests of the famous brotherhood of Rā, the Sun-god, who had made their head-quarters in Egypt at Ȧnnu, i.e., On, or Heliopolis. The old native beliefs of the country were of a more material character than the doctrines which the priests of Heliopolis taught, but it was found impossible to eradicate them from the minds of the people, and the priests therefore framed religious works in such a manner that they might be acceptable both to those who believed in the old animal-gods, tree-gods, plant-gods, &c., of Egypt, and those who preferred a purely solar cult, such as that of the worship of the Sun-god Rā. The oldest Books of the Dead, in fact, represent the compromise arrived at under the IVth, Vth, and VIth Dynasties, between the priests of the old and the new religions. This being so, the religious texts of the period represent too much a patch-work belief for purposes of systematic illustration, and in the result, and perhaps also through the funeral customs of the day, the growth in men's minds of the wish for illustrated guides to the Underworld was retarded.

When the glory of sovereignty departed from the kings who held court at Memphis after the end of the rule of the VIth Dynasty, the system of solar theology, which had been promulgated in Lower Egypt by the priests of Heliopolis, began to make its way into Upper Egypt, and wherever it came it assumed a leading position among the religious systems of the day. The kings of the VIIth and VIIIth Dynasties, like those of the IIIrd, IVth, and VIth, came from Memphis, but they had comparatively little power in the land, and, so far as we know, they did not build for themselves pyramids for tombs, and there is no evidence forthcoming to show that they filled the walls of their sepulchres with religious texts. They carried on neither wars nor building operations of any importance, and it seems that their tombs were neither large nor magnificent. Owing to their feeble rule the governors of Suten-ḥenen, or Herakleopolis, and those who ruled in the provinces near that city, succeeded in gaining their independence, and the kings of the IXth and Xth Dynasties were Herakleopolitans; their rule gradually extended to the south, and the religious influence of their priests was so great that they succeeded in forcing many of their mythological legends and beliefs into the accepted religion of the country, and these subsequently became part and parcel of the great Recension of the Theban Book of the Dead. The dominion of the Herakleopolitans, however, was of comparatively short duration, and it collapsed under the attacks of the bold and vigorous governors of the Thebaïd, whose capital was at Thebes. Judging from the historical evidence concerning the period which lies between the VIth and the XIth Dynasties, neither the two last Memphitic nor the two Herakleopolitan Dynasties of kings did anything to improve the general condition of the country, and it seems as if they found it necessary to employ all their energies to maintain their position and the little real power in the country which they possessed.

As this was the case, we need not wonder that all magnificence disappeared from funeral rites and ceremonies, and that the tombs of the period were small and unimportant. The gods were worshipped and the dead were buried as matters of course, but it goes without saying that kings, whose authority was not consolidated, and whose power was ineffective except in the immediate neighbourhood of the towns in which they lived, who were unable to wage wars in Syria and Sinai and to bring back much spoil, could neither establish Colleges of priests nor endow new temples; for in ancient Egypt, as elsewhere, the fortunes of the gods and the wealth of their sanctuaries increased or declined according as the inhabitants of the land were prosperous or otherwise. Similarly also, when the community was suffering from the evil effects of a long period of civil wars, and business was at a standstill, and farmers were unable to carry on the usual agricultural operations on which both the government and the priesthood ultimately depended for support, it was impossible for men to bury their dead with all the pomp and ceremony which were the characteristics of funerals in times of peace and prosperity. The innate conservatism of the Egyptians made them cling to their ancient beliefs during this period of stress, but no important pyramids were built, and very few private funeral chapels were maintained at expensive rates, and the souls of the dead were committed to such protection as could be obtained by the prayers of their relatives and friends, and by the utterance of religious formulae, and by inexpensive amulets.

With the rise to power of the Princes of Thebes, things took a turn for the better so far as worship in the temples and the care for the dead were concerned. So soon as they had overcome their enemies the Princes of Herakleopolis, and their confederates the Princes of Asyût, and had firmly established themselves on the throne of Egypt, they sent men to reopen the quarries in the First Cataract and in the Wâdî Ḥammâmât near Coptos. This is a sure proof that the new line of kings, most of whom bear the name of Menthu-ḥetep, had need of large quantities of granite, and of sandstone of various kinds, and such materials can only have been required for the building of temples and palaces, and funeral altars and stelae, sarcophagi, &c. The fact that the work was begun again in the quarries also proves that the authority of the Menthu-ḥeteps was well established. Menthu-ḥetep II., we are told by an inscription set up in the Wadî Ḥammâmât by his officer Åmen-em-ḥāt, caused to be quarried a block of stone which measured eight cubits, by four cubits, by two cubits, i.e., about thirteen feet six inches long, six feet six inches wide, and three feet six inches thick, and it is probable that he required this for a sarcophagus. This king is also famous as the maker of a well in the desert, the mouth of which was about sixteen feet six inches square; and at one time he employed several thousands of men, including three thousand carriers or boatmen, in his stone-works. His successor, Menthu-ḥetep III., continued the work in the quarries, and built himself a pyramid, called Khu-ȧst, , in the mountain of Tchesert at Thebes, which may now be identified with that portion of the great Theban cemetery to which the name Dêr al-Baḥarî was given by the Arabic-speaking Egyptians.

This building is mentioned in the great Abbott Papyrus preserved in the British Museum (No. 10,221), where it is declared to have been found unviolated by the members of the Commission which was appointed to inquire into the condition of the royal tombs, after the robberies which had taken place in them about the period of the rule of the priest-kings of Thebes, B.C. 1,000. The remains of the tomb of Menthu-ḥetep III. have been recently discovered,[1] and though at the time of writing it has not been completely excavated, sufficient has been done to show that it is a very remarkable building. It is clear that the lower part of it is rectangular, and that it was surrounded by a colonnade; the outside is cased with limestone slabs, behind which is a "wall of rough and heavy nodules

[1] See a letter in the *Times* of June 22nd, 1905 (p. 4), on the "Most Ancient Temple at Thebes," by Prof. E. Naville and Mr. H. R. Hall.

of flint, and the middle is filled with rubbish and loose stones." On this rectangular building, or base, a small pyramid probably stood, at least, this is what we should expect. The remains already excavated prove that this base was surrounded by a triple row of columns, which supported a ceiling and formed a hypostyle passage or colonnade, which "must have been quite "dark, or nearly so (like the ambulatories surrounding "the shrines in later temples), for the outside was "closed by a thick wall." Between this wall and the edge of the platform on which the building stood was an outer colonnade of square pillars, but the pillars no longer exist. In the rock below the pavement of this colonnade a number of tombs were hewn; each consisted of a pit from twelve to fifteen feet deep, which led to a small rectangular chamber, wherein originally stood a limestone sarcophagus. In these tombs women who were both priestesses of Hathor and members of the royal *harîm* were buried, and further excavations will no doubt reveal the fact that Menthu-ḥetep's high officers of state were buried in somewhat similar tombs in the immediate neighbourhood of the remarkable monument which the Egypt Exploration Fund has brought to light through the exertions of Prof. E. Naville and Mr. H. R. Hall.

The facts given above indicate that Menthu-ḥetep III. built a splendid tomb at Thebes, and it seems that in certain particulars he copied the royal pyramid tombs of the IVth, Vth, and VIth Dynasties. It is unlikely that the superstructure which he set upon the rectangular base, to which reference has been made above, and which is assumed to have been in the form of a pyramid, was as large as any of the important pyramids of Gîza, and the base on which it rested is "a "new and interesting fact in Egyptian architecture"; but when he set his funeral monument on the rocky platform in the mountain of Tchesert it is more than probable that either he or his architect had in mind the rocky platform on which the great Pyramids of Gîza stand, and it seems as if he built it on a massive rectangular base, so that it might appear conspicuous and imposing from a distance. Like the earlier royal builders of pyramids, Menthu-ḥetep built a funeral temple in connexion with his pyramid, and established an order of priests, who were to perform the services and ceremonies connected with his worship, and he allowed the ladies of his court to be buried round about it, just as did the kings of old who reigned at Memphis. The great feature of Menthu-ḥetep's monument, which has no parallel in the older pyramids in the north of Egypt, is the ramp, with a double row of square columns on each side of it, which he built on the front or eastern face of the temple platform.

Now whilst Menthu-ḥetep III. was employed in building his pyramid and funeral temple, the hereditary governors and nobles of important provinces in Upper Egypt were not slow to avail themselves of the opportunity which peace and the renewed prosperity of the country gave them, and they began to make rock-hewn tombs for themselves and the members of their families in the hills, and to cause their bodies to be buried in elaborately inscribed or painted wooden coffins. Of coffins of this period, one of the oldest examples is that of ÅMAMU , which was purchased by the Trustees of the British Museum so long ago as 1834.[1] On the inside of this coffin is inscribed in black ink in the hieratic character a series of texts which are extracts from the Heliopolitan Recension of the Book of the Dead; these are enclosed within a coloured border, formed of rectangles, painted in blue, green, yellow, and red. Above the texts are carefully drawn, and painted as nearly as possible in their natural colours, representations of most of the objects which the deceased hoped he would use in the Underworld, and these pictures prove that the knowledge of the elaborate funeral rites and ceremonies, which were observed at Memphis under the IVth Dynasty, had descended in a complete state to the period when Åmamu's coffin was made and ornamented.

In connection with Åmamu's coffin reference must be made to a large group of coffins which was excavated a few years ago at Al-Barsha, a place situated on the north side of a rocky valley, just behind the modern Coptic village of Dêr An-Nakhla, near Shêkh Abâda

[1] See Birch, *Ancient Egyptian Texts from the Coffin of Amamu in the British Museum*, London, 1886.

(the ancient Antinoë), in Upper Egypt. All the coffins found here are rectangular in shape, and have so much in common with the coffin of Ȧmamu, in respect of shape, and in the arrangement of their texts and pictures, including the representations of *maṣṭaba* doors, that it seems impossible to assign to them a date much earlier or later than the period of the XIth Dynasty. For our present purpose, however, whatever be their exact date, they are of the greatest importance, for on the insides of the panels of some of them are painted the oldest known illustrations of certain sections of Books of the Dead. The texts inscribed on them contain extracts from the Heliopolitan Recension of the Book of the Dead, of which we know so much from the selections given in the Pyramids of Unȧs, Tetȧ, and other kings, but side by side with these are copies of chapters belonging to Books of the Dead, which seem to have been originally composed at some anterior period, and which were intended to reflect the more popular and more materialistic religious views and beliefs. Among such books must be mentioned the "Book of Two Ways," or the "Two Ways of the Blessed Dead," of which a version inscribed on a coffin in the Berlin Museum has been recently published.[1] The rubrical directions of this work show that it was compiled when implicit belief existed in the minds of the Egyptians as to the efficacy of

[1] Schack-Schackenburg, *Das Buch von den Zwei Wegen des Seligen Toten*, Leipzig, 1903.

certain "words of power" (*ḥekau*, ) and of pictures of the gods, and it is clear that many portions of it are purely magical, and were intended to produce very material results. Thus concerning one passage a rubric says, "Whosoever knoweth this "Chapter may have union with women by night or "by day, and the heart (or, desire) of the woman shall "come to him whensoever he would enjoy her." This rubric follows a text[1] in which the deceased is made to pray for power of generation similar to that possessed by the god Beba, and for the will and opportunity of overcoming women, and it was to be written on a bandlet which was to be attached to the right arm. Moreover, the soul which had knowledge of certain sections of the work would "live among the living ones," and would "see Osiris every day," and would have "air in his nostrils, and death would never draw nigh unto him."[2] The illustrations which accompany the texts on the coffins from Al-Barsha make it evident that under the XIth Dynasty the Egyptian theologian had not only divided the Underworld in his mind into sections, with doors, &c., but that he was prepared to describe that portion of it which belonged to the blessed dead, and to supply a plan of it! Besides the sections from the "Pyramid Texts," to which reference has already been made, and the "Book of the Two Ways," the coffins of Al-Barsha

[1] **See page 49, l. 9—p. 51, l. 11.** [2] **See page 49, ll. 4—9.**

contain a number of texts of various lengths, many of which have titles, and resemble in form the Chapters of the great Theban Recension of the Book of the Dead. Examples of these have been published in Prof. Maspero's *Recueil de Travaux*, tom. xxvi., p. 64 ff., by M. P. Lacau, e.g., "Chapter of the Seven Addresses of homage to the goddess Meḥ-urt"; [Chapter of] "the reassembling of the kinsfolk of a man in Neter-khert"; "Chapter of driving back Ḳebḳa"; "Chapter of setting out for Orion," &c.

From the considerations set forth above it is quite clear that the practice of illustrating certain sections of Books of the Dead existed under the XIth Dynasty, and there is no good reason for doubting that it continued to be observed during the prosperous rule of the kings of the XIIth Dynasty. Under the IVth, Vth, and VIth Dynasties the selections of extracts from Books of the Dead which were intended to benefit royal souls in the Underworld were cut upon the walls of the chambers and corridors of their pyramids, and in the case of private individuals texts intended to produce the same effect were usually cut into the walls of the chambers wherein their stone sarcophagi were placed. The pyramids of the kings of the XIth and XIIth Dynasties, whether in the north or south of Egypt, are not, so far as the information at present available goes, characterized by lengthy extracts from Books of the Dead, and officials and men of rank in general were content to dispense with the cutting of religious inscriptions into the sides of stone sarcophagi, and into the walls of the passages and chambers of their tombs in the mountains, and to transfer them to the sides of their brightly painted, rectangular wooden coffins. The practical advantages of this change are obvious. Wooden coffins were easier to obtain and cheaper than stone sarcophagi, longer and fuller selections from religious texts could be easily and quickly traced upon them in the hieratic character, which an expert scribe could, no doubt, write at a rapid rate, the expense of adding coloured drawings was small, and, above all, the deceased would have close to his mummy the sacred writings on which he so greatly relied for assistance in the Other World. The coffin which was fully inscribed could easily be made to hold copies of all the texts deemed to be of vital importance to the dead, and such a coffin when, as was frequently the case, it was placed in a massive, outer, wooden coffin, served the purpose of the large rolls of papyri inscribed with religious and funeral texts, and illustrated with elaborately painted vignettes, which were buried with the dead from the XVIIIth to the XXVIth Dynasty.

After the death of Ȧmen-em-ḥāt III., who was perhaps the greatest king of the XIIth Dynasty, the whole country fell into a state of confusion, and the kings of Thebes ceased to be masters of all Egypt. The kings of the XIIIth Dynasty were Theban and reigned at Thebes, and appear to have maintained their hold in a considerable degree upon Upper Egypt; but the kings of the XIVth Dynasty reigned at Xoïs, in the Delta, and many of them were contemporaries of the kings in Upper Egypt. The kings of the XVth and XVIth Dynasties were Hyksos, or "Shepherd Kings," and their rule was overthrown by Seqenen-Rā III., a king of the XVIIth Dynasty, and a Theban, probably about B.C. 1800. In the interval between the XIIth and the XVIIIth Dynasties the ceremonies connected with the worship of the gods in their temples, and the funerals of kings and officials, lost the magnificence which had characterized them under the XIIth Dynasty, and the building of pyramids and the making of rock-hewn tombs ceased for a period of some hundreds of years. With the rise to power of the Theban kings, who formed the XVIIIth Dynasty, a marvellous development of temple and funeral ceremonies took place, and, thanks chiefly to the vast quantities of spoil which were poured into Thebes by the victorious armies of Egypt on their return from Western Asia, the cult of the gods and of the dead assumed proportions which it had never reached before in Egypt.

The chief deity of Thebes was Ȧmen, the "Hidden," or perhaps "unknown," god, in whose honour a shrine was built to the north of the city, in a place called "Ap," or "Apt," by the Egyptians, and "Karnak" by the modern inhabitants of Luxor. It is impossible to say at present exactly when the first sanctuary of this god was built at Thebes, but the discovery of the large collection of 457 votive statues of kings and officials and other objects, made by M. Legrain[1] in 1901-2, indicates that the foundation of the sanctuary of Åmen dates from a very early period of Dynastic History.[2] Be this as it may, the god Åmen seems to have enjoyed no special importance or popularity in Egypt until the XIIth Dynasty, when his sanctuary appears to have been rebuilt and enlarged; but so long as his priests were dependent for maintenance upon the revenues of Upper Egypt alone neither they nor their god can have enjoyed any very great wealth. When Seqenen-Rā III. defeated the Hyksos, and made himself master of all Egypt, and when Åāhmes I. (Amasis) drove the Hyksos out from their stronghold Avaris, in the Delta, thus completing the work of the deliverance of the country from a foreign yoke, which Seqenen-Rā III. had begun, they attributed the success of their arms to their god Åmen, who was from this time forward regarded not only as the principal god of the Egyptians, but as the "king of the gods." Soon after Åmen-ḥetep I., the successor of Åāhmes I., came to the throne, he made war against the Nubians, and became master of the gold-producing districts of the Eastern Sûdân. His next care was to rebuild, or perhaps to repair and add to, the sanctuary

[1] See Maspero's *Recueil de Travaux*, tom. xxvii., p. 67.

[2] According to M. Legrain, the IIIrd Dynasty (*Recueil*, tom. xxvii., p. 67).

of Åmen, and he founded the famous College of priests of Åmen, whose counsels guided, both for good and for evil, the destinies of Egypt for several hundreds of years. He richly endowed these priests and their god and his temple, and on many of the coffins of this brotherhood are representations of members of the order in the act of worshipping his names, and of pouring out libations before his cartouches. The priests of Åmen had, no doubt, good reason for worshipping Åmen-ḥetep with such devotion.

It is unnecessary to describe in detail the growth of the cult of Åmen under the XVIIIth Dynasty, and it will suffice to say that the history of his cult is, practically, the history of Egypt for nearly one thousand years. His priests made him possessor of the principal attributes and titles of all the ancient gods of Egypt, and their absolute power enabled them to modify the old systems of belief of the country. They introduced the primitive gods of the land into their own system of theology, but assigned to them subordinate positions and powers inferior to those of Åmen, or Åmen-Rā, as he was called, and the new editions of most of the old religious works which appeared at Thebes bore the traces of having been edited in accordance with their views and opinions. In many of its aspects the cult of Åmen was less material than that of many of the old gods, and the religion of the priests themselves ruthlessly rejected many of the primitive beliefs which survived among the populace in general. They were obliged to tolerate and respect the universal belief in Osiris as the judge, king, and god of the dead, for they, of course, found it impossible to eliminate from the minds of the people the effect which the traditions of a material heaven, handed down for untold generations, had made upon them. Among the servants of Àmen and his temple, however, there were some who preferred to put their faith in the religious writings which had satisfied their ancestors many centuries before, and to these we owe the great collection of religious and funeral texts called PER EM HRU, "[The Book of] Coming forth by Day," which is now commonly known as the Theban Recension of the Book of the Dead.

It is true that the subject matter of many of the texts is older than the IVth Dynasty, and that the phraseology of some dates from the period of the Vth and VIth Dynasties, and that the forms in which most of them are cast are not more recent than the XIth or XIIth Dynasty, but it is equally true that the editing and arrangement of them by the Theban priests, to say nothing of the addition of supplementary hymns, Chapters, and coloured illustrations, produced a very decided change in the general teachings of the collection.

"The Book of Coming Forth by Day," in its Theban form, was an illustrated guide to the kingdom of Osiris, but its teachings did not satisfy the strict followers of Àmen-Rā, and they brought into use a Recension of a work in which they were able to promulgate the particular ideas of their order as to the future state of the dead. The followers of Osiris believed that the righteous dead would find their everlasting abode in the kingdom of that god, and would enjoy in a fertile land, with running streams, a life very like that which the well-to-do Egyptian lived upon earth. The followers of Åmen-Rā aimed at securing a place in the boat of the Sun-god, i.e., the "Boat of Millions of Years," so that they might sail over the sky with him each day, and enjoy the sight of the earth on which they had lived, and might, under his all-powerful protection, pass through the regions of darkness by night, and emerge in heaven, being reborn each day. In the kingdom of Osiris the beatified dead ate bread-cakes made from one wonderful kind of grain, and drank beer made from another kind, and enjoyed conjugal intercourse, and the company of their relations and friends; all their material comforts were supplied by the use of words of power, &c., by which they even obtained entrance into that kingdom.

Entrance to the Boat of Millions of Years was likewise obtained by the knowledge of magical words and formulae, and of the secret names of the great gods, but the food on which lived the beatified souls who succeeded in securing a place in the Boat consisted of the emanations of the god Rā, or, according to the priests of Åmen, Åmen-Rā. In other words, the beatified souls in the Boat became beings formed of the light of Rā, on which they subsisted. The belief that the souls of the righteous flew into the Boat of Rā is a very old one, but the doctrine in the form in which it was developed by the priests of Åmen can never have been universally accepted in Egypt, for it was not sufficiently material to satisfy any but the educated classes. The great kings of the XVIIIth and XIXth Dynasties, being convinced that their military successes were due to the influence and operation of Åmen-Rā, dutifully accepted the instructions of the priests of the god in all matters relating to his worship, and they permitted them to prepare tombs for them in the Valley of Bîbân al-Mulûk at Thebes, which were built and ornamented according to the views held by the followers of Åmen-Rā concerning the Other World. The oldest tombs here, i.e., those of the XVIIIth Dynasty, are usually entered by means of long, sloping corridors that lead down into the the chambers which held the sarcophagi, and into smaller halls which adjoin the large chambers; in the later tombs the corridors are often very long, and it is this characteristic which caused certain Greek writers to call them Σύριγγες, i.e., "shepherd's pipes." Of the forty-five tombs in this valley (Strabo mentions forty only), the oldest royal tomb appears to be that of Thothmes I., and the most recent that of Rameses XII., of the XXth Dynasty. These tombs vary greatly in details, just as they do in size and in the arrangement and number of their chambers, but it seems that each tomb was intended to represent the Underworld, and that the ceremonies, which were performed in it as the mummy was taken from the entrance to the last chamber in which it was to rest, were highly symbolical, and that the progress of the body through the tomb was, so far as it was possible, made to resemble that of the Sun-god through the hours of the night in the Other World.

The religious texts with which the walls of the royal tombs are decorated do not consist of extracts from the funeral works of the Ancient and Middle Empires, but of sections from a work entitled ÀM-ṬUAT, i.e., [The Book of] "what is in the Ṭuat," or Underworld, and many of these are illustrated more or less fully with coloured pictures of the gods, mythological scenes, &c. The rubrics show that portions of this work belong to remote antiquity, and many of the beliefs which appear in it are the products of the period when the Egyptians were partly, if not wholly, savages. In the book itself numbers of gods and mythological beings are mentioned whose names are not found elsewhere in Egyptian literature. As we find it in the tombs of the royal followers of Àmen, the Book "Àm-Ṭuat" contains all the dogmas and doctrines which the priests of Àmen held concerning the future life and the state and condition of the dead, and it is quite easy to see that the great object of those who compiled it was to prove that Àmen-Rā was not only the head of the gods in heaven, and the ruler of the world which he had created, but also the king of all the gods of the dead, and the master of all the beings who were in the

Underworld. In other words, the priests of Åmen asserted the absolute sovereignty of their god, and their own religious supremacy. It is, however, interesting to note that certain kings did not entirely shake off their belief in Osiris, and in the efficacy of the Chapters of the Book of Coming Forth by Day, for Thothmes III. was swathed in a linen sheet on which was written a copy of the CLIVth Chapter, and Åmenḥetep III. was rolled up in sheets whereon extracts from several Chapters of that work were inscribed. Seti I. went a good deal further, for although fully illustrated copies of Divisions I.—XI. of the Book "Åm-Tuat" were painted on the walls of his tomb, he took care to have a complete copy of the Book of Gates,[1] with full illustrations, and copies of the LXXIInd and LXXXIXth Chapters of the Book of Coming Forth by Day cut on his alabaster sarcophagus.

The Chapter which Thothmes III. believed to be all-powerful is entitled "Chapter of not letting the body perish," and if its words really express his convictions, he must have been terrified at the idea of his material body falling into dust and decay, and must have hoped for its resurrection through Osiris. The Chapters which Seti I. had cut on his sarcophagus are entitled the "Chapter of Coming Forth by Day, and of making a way through Åmmeḥet," and the "Chapter of causing the soul to be united to its body in the Underworld." In the former he declares that

[1] See within, Chapter IV., p. 85.

he knows the names of the gods who preside over the Other World, and also the proper words of power, and because he has this knowledge he demands admission into Sekhet-Åaru, a portion of Osiris's kingdom of Sekhet-ḥetepet, and a constant and abundant supply of wheat (for bread), barley (for beer), incense, unguents, &c., and the power to assume any form he pleases at will. In the latter he calls upon certain gods to make his soul rejoin its body, and, addressing the gods who tow the Boat of Millions of Years, he asks them to cause him to be born from the womb of the Sky-goddess Nut in the eastern horizon of heaven, [daily,] for ever.

It has already been said that a complete illustrated copy of the Book of Gates was also inscribed on the sarcophagus of Seti I., and it is not easy to explain this fact until we remember the important position which it makes Osiris to hold in the Other World. That the book is formed of very ancient materials is evident from the last sections, which certainly contain magical texts and pictures specially prepared with the object of making the sun to rise, and there is little doubt that the latter are representations of the ceremonies which the primitive Egyptians actually performed to produce that most desirable effect. The earlier sections of the Book are full of magical ideas, but scattered among them are expressions of beliefs which, it seems, must belong to a later period of civilization, and passages which impress the reader with the idea that they were composed by men who believed that the righteous would be rewarded and the wicked punished in the world to come. Special prominence is given to the conception of the Judgment, wherein Osiris is the Judge of the dead. As the result of this Judgment the righteous have allotments of land meted out to them, which vary in size according to their deserts, and the wicked are slain, and their bodies cut in pieces, and their souls destroyed. In many particualrs the views of the Book of Gates concerning the future state agree closely with those of the Book of Coming Forth by Day.

The net result of the facts stated in the last two paragraphs proves that Seti I. relied for salvation upon the protection, part magical and part religious, afforded by the sacred writings of two great schools of religious thought, the leaders of which in his day preached opposing and contradictory doctrines. It may be argued that by filling the walls of his tomb and sarcophagus with the texts of such books he was merely acting from the point of view of religious expediency, wishing to indicate his impartiality in respect of the followers of Ȧmen and the followers of Osiris, and his respect for the ancient traditional beliefs, however material, crude, and impossible they may have appeared to him personally. This, however, is unlikely to have been the case, and it is far more probable that he believed every religious or funeral text to have its own special value as a means of salvation, and that he selected for inscribing on the walls of his tomb and sarcophagus those which he thought would be the most likely to secure for him in the next world an existence which would be at once happy and everlasting. Therefore Seti I. provided himself with amulets, *ushabtiu* figures, magical formulae, pictures of gods and fiends to be used in working sympathetic magic, religious formulae and copies of hymns and funeral works, an inscribed tomb and sarcophagus, &c.; in fact, he was painfully anxious to omit nothing from the inscriptions in his tomb which would propitiate any god, or appease the wrath and turn aside the opposition of any of the fiends wherewith he had filled his Underworld.

CHAPTER II.

THE EARLIEST EGYPTIAN CONCEPTION OF THE OTHER WORLD.

HAVING briefly referred to the origin and development of the magical, religious, and purely funeral texts which, sometimes with and sometimes without illustrations, formed the "Guides" to the Ancient Egyptian Underworld, the form of the conceptions concerning the place of departed spirits as it appears in the Recensions of the XVIIIth and XIXth Dynasties must now be considered. To reconstruct the form which they took in the Predynastic Period is impossible, for no materials exist, and the documents of the Early Empire are concerned chiefly with providing the deceased with an abundance of meat, drink, and other material comforts, and numbers of wives and concubines, and a place in Sekhet-Åaru, a division of Sekhet-ḥetepet, to which the name "Elysian Fields" has not inaptly been given. In later times Sekhet-Åaru, or Sekhet-Åanru, comprised all Sekhet-ḥetepet. Of Sekhet-ḥetepet as a whole the earliest known pictures are those which are painted on the coffins of

Al-Barsha, and of no portion of this region have we any detailed illustrations of the occupations of its inhabitants older than the XVIIIth Dynasty. To the consideration of Sekhet-Åaru, which was the true heaven of every faithful worshipper of Osiris, from the time when he became the judge and benevolent god and friend of the dead down to the Ptolemaïc Period, that is to say, for a period of four thousand years at least, the scribes and artists of the XVIIIth Dynasty devoted much attention, and the results of their views are set forth in the copies of PER-EM-HRU, or the Theban Book of the Dead, which have come down to us.

In one of the oldest copies of PER-EM-HRU, i.e., in the Papyrus of Nu,[1] is a vignette of the Seven *Ārits*, or divisions of Sekhet-Åaru; the portion shown of each *Ārit* is the door, or gate, which is guarded by a gatekeeper, by a watcher, who reports the arrival of every comer, and by a herald, who receives and announces his name. All these beings save two have the head of an animal, or bird, on a human body, a fact which indicates the great antiquity of the ideas that underlie this vignette. Their names are:—

Ārit	I.	*Gatekeeper.*	SEKHET-ḤRÅ-ĀSHT-ÅRU.
		Watcher.	SEMETU.
		Herald.	HU-KHERU.

[1] British Museum, No. 10,477, sheet 26 (Chapter cxliv.).

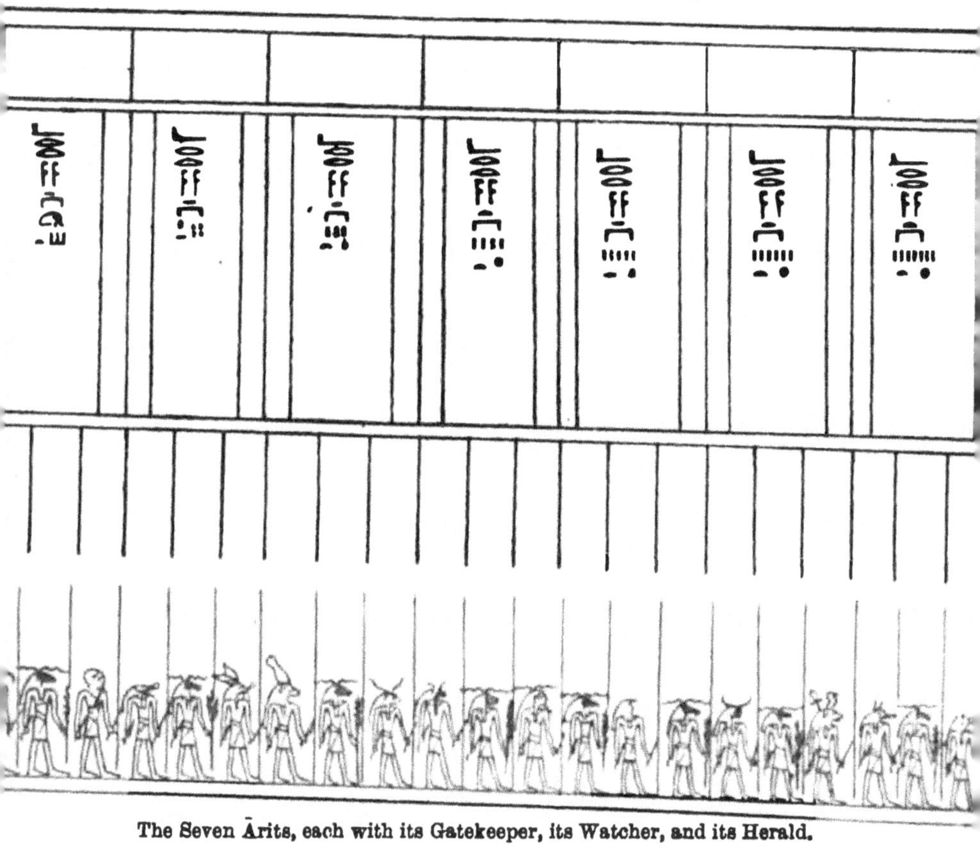

The Seven Ārits, each with its Gatekeeper, its Watcher, and its Herald.

Arit II.	*Gatekeeper.*	ṬUN-ḤĀT.
	Watcher.	SEQEṬ-ḤRÅ.
	Herald.	SABES.
Arit III.	*Gatekeeper.*	ÅM-ḤUAT-ENT-PEḤUI-FI.
	Watcher.	RES-ḤRÅ.
	Herald.	UĀAU.
Arit IV.	*Gatekeeper.*	KHESEF-ḤRÅ-ĀSHT-KHERU. .
	Watcher.	RES-ÅB.
	Herald.	NETEḲA-ḤRÅ-KHESEF-AṬU.
Ārit V.	*Gatekeeper.*	ĀNKH-EM-FENṬU.
	Watcher.	ASHEBU.
	Herald.	ṬEB-ḤER-KEHAAT.
Arit VI.	*Gatekeeper.*	ÅKEN-TAU-K-HA-KHERU.
	Watcher.	ÅN-ḤRÅ.
	Herald.	METES-ḤRÅ-ÅRI-SHE.
Ārit VII.	*Gatekeeper.*	MEṬES-SEN.
	Watcher.	ÅĀA-KHERU.
	Herald.	KHESEF-ḤRÅ-KHEMIU.

From another place in the same papyrus,[1] and from other papyri, we learn that the "Secret Gates of the House of Osiris in Sekhet-Åaru" were twenty-one in number; the Chapter (CXLVI.) gives the name of each Gate, and also that of each Gatekeeper up to No. X., thus:—

I. *Gate.* NEBT-SEṬAU-QAT-SEBT-ḤERT-NEBT-KHEBKHEBT-SERT-MEṬU-

[1] Sheet 25.

KHESEFET-NESHENIU-NEḤEMET-UAI-EN-I-UAU.

Gatekeeper. NERI.

II. *Gate.* NEBT-PET-ḤENT-TAUI-NESBIT-NEBT-TEMEMU-TENT-BU-NEBU.

Gatekeeper. MES-PEḤ (or, MES-PTAḤ).

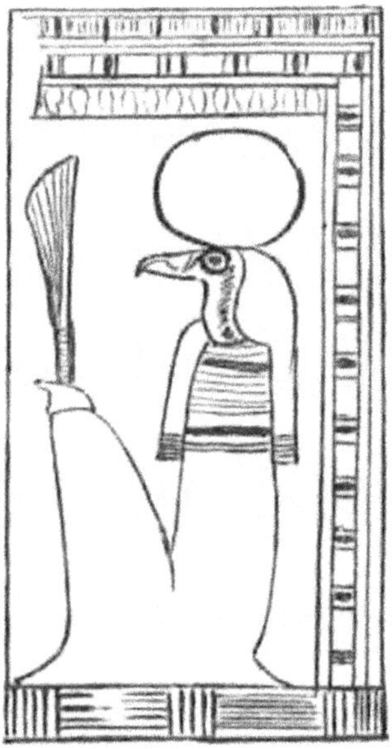

Gate I.

Gate II.

III. *Gate.* NEBT-KHAUT-ĀAT-ĀABET-SENETCHEMET-NETER-NEB-ȦM-S-HRU-KHENT-ER-ȦBṬU.

Gatekeeper. ERTĀT-SEBANQA.

IV. *Gate.* SEKHEMET-ṬESU-ḤENT-TAUI-ḤETCHET-KHEFTI-NU-URṬ-ȦB-ȦRIT-SARU-SHUT-EM-ĀU.

Gatekeeper. NEḲAU.

Gate III.

Gate IV.

V. *Gate.* NEBT - REKHU - RESHT - TEBHET - ṬĀTU - NES - ȦN - ĀQ - ERES - UN - ṬEP-F.

Gatekeeper. ḤENTI-REQU.

Gate V.

Gate VI.

VI. *Gate.* NEBT-SENKET-ĀAT-HEMHEMET-ÅN-REKH-TU-QA-S-ER-USEKH-S-ÅN-QEMTU-QEṬ-S-EM-SHAĀ-ÅU-ḤEFU-ḤER-S-ÅN-REKH-TENNU-MES-EN-THU-KHER-ḤĀT-URṬU-ÅB.

Gatekeeper. SMAMTI.

Gate VII.

Gate VIII.

VII. *Gate.* ÅKKIT-ḤEBSET-BAḲ-AAKEBIT-MERT-SEḤAP-KHAT.

Gatekeeper. ÅKENTI.

VIII. *Gate.* REKḤET-BESU-ĀKHMET-TCHAFU-SEPṬ-PĀU-KHAT-ṬET-SMAM-ÅN-NETCHNETCH-ÅTET-SESH-ḤER-S-EN-SENṬ-NÅH-S.

Gatekeeper. KHU-TCHET-F.

IX. *Gate.* ȦMT-ḤĀT-NEBT-USER-HERT-ȦB-MESTET-NEB-S-KHEMT-SHAĀ-.....-EM-SHEN-S-SATU-EM-UATCHET-QEMĀ-THESET-BES-ḤEBSET-BAḲ-FEQAT-NEB-S-RĀ-NEB.

Gatekeeper. TCHESEF.

Gate IX.

Gate X.

X. *Gate.* QAT-KHERU-NEHESET-ṬENȦTU-SEBḤET-ER-QA-EN-KHERU-S-NERT-NEBT-SHEFSHEFT-ȦN-ṬER-S-NETET-EM-KHENNU-S.

Gatekeeper. SEKHEN-UR.

XI. *Gate.* NEMT-ṬESU-UBṬET-SEBȦU-ḤENT-ENT-SEBKHET-NEBT-ȦRU-NES-ȦHEHI-HRU-EN-ȦNKHEKH.[1]

[1] The names of the gatekeepers of Gates XI.—XXI. are not given in the papyri.

XII. *Gate.* NAST-TAUI-SI-SEKSEKET-NEMMÅTU-EM-NEHEPU-QAḤIT-NEBT-KHU-SETEMTH-KHERU-NEB-S.

XIII. *Gate.* STA-EN-ÅSÅR-ĀÅUI-F-ḤER-S-SEḤETCHET-ḤĀP-EM-ÅMENT-F.

XIV. *Gate.* NEBT-ṬENṬEN-KHEBT-ḤER-ṬESHERU-ÅRU-NES-HAKER-HRU-EN-SETEMET-ĀU.

XV. *Gate.* BAṬI-ṬESHERU-QEMḤUT-ÅARERT-PERT-EM-ḲERḤ-SENTCHERT-SEBÅ-ḤER-QABI-F-ERṬĀT-ĀÅUI-S-EN-URṬU-ÅB-EM-ÅT-F-ÅRT-ITET-SHEM-S.

XVI. *Gate.* NERUTET-NEBT-ÅAṬET-KHAĀ-KHAU-EM-BA-EN-RETH-KHEBSU-MIT-EN-RETH-SERT-PER-QEMAMET-SHĀṬ.

XVII. *Gate.* KHEBT-ḤER-SENF-ÅḤIBIT-NEBT-UAUIUAIT.

XVIII. *Gate.* MER-SETAU-ĀB-ÅBTU-MERER-S-SHĀṬ-ṬEPU-AMKHIT-NEBT-AḤĀ-UḤSET-SEBÅU-EM-MĀSHERU.

XIX. *Gate.* SERT-NEHEPU-EM-ĀḤĀ-S-URSH-SHEMMET-NEBT-USERU-ANU-EN-TEḤUTI-TCHESEF.

XX. *Gate.* AMT-KHEN-TEPEḤ-NEB-S-ḤEBS-REN-S-ÅMENT-QEMAMU-S-THETET-ḤĀTI-EN-ÅM-S.

XXI. *Gate.* ṬEM-SIA-ER-MEṬUU-ÅRI-ḤEMEN-HAI-NEBÅU-S.

From the above lists, and from copies of them which are found in the Papyrus of Ani, and other finely illustrated Books of the Dead, it is quite clear that, according to one view, Sekhet-Ȧaru, the land of the blessed, was divided into seven sections, each of which was entered through a Gate having three attendants, and that, according to other traditions, it had sections varying in number from ten to twenty-one, for each of the Gates mentioned above must have been intended to protect a division. It will be noted that the names of the Ten Gates are in reality long sentences, which make sense and can be translated, but there is little doubt that under the XVIIIth Dynasty these sentences were used as purely magical formulae, or words of power, which, provided the deceased knew how to pronounce them, there was no great need to understand. In other words, it was not any goodness or virtue of his own which would enable him to pass through the Gates of Sekhet-Ȧaru, and disarm the opposition of their warders, but the knowledge of certain formulæ, or words of power, and magical names. We are thus taken back to a very remote period by these ideas, and to a time when the conceptions as to the abode of the blessed were of a purely magical character; the addition of pictures to the formulae, or names, belongs to a later period, when it was thought right to strengthen them by illustrations. The deceased, who not only possessed the secret name of a god or demon, but also a picture of him whereby he could easily recognize him when he met him, was doubly armed against danger.

In addition to the Seven Ārits, and the Ten, Fourteen, or Twenty-one Gates (according to the manuscript authority followed), the Sekhet-Ḥetepet possessed Fourteen or Fifteen Ȧats, or Regions, each of which was presided over by a god. Their names, as given in the Papyrus of Nu,[1] are as follows:—

Ȧat I. AMENTET, wherein a man lived on cakes and ale; its god was ȦMSU-QEṬ, or MENU-QEṬ.

Ȧat II. SEKHET-ȦARU. Its walls are of iron. The wheat here is five cubits high, the barley

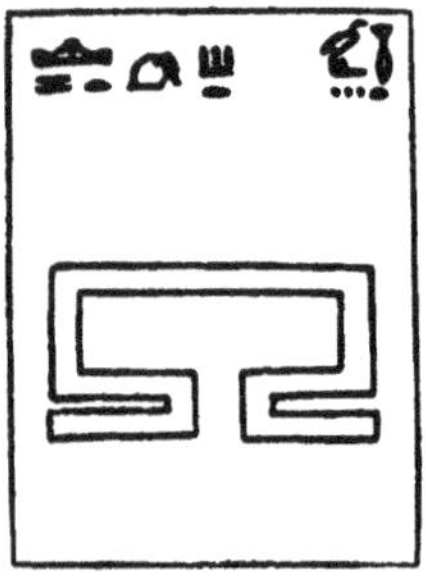

Aat I.

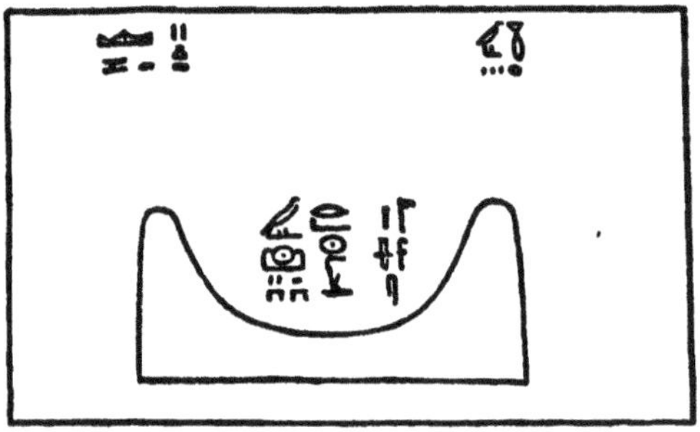

Ȧat II.

is seven cubits high, and the Spirits who reap them are nine cubits high. The god of this Ȧat is RĀ-ḤERUKHUTI.

Ȧat III. ȦATENKHU. Its god was OSIRIS or RĀ.

Ȧat IV. ṬUI-QAUI-ĀȦUI. Its god was SATI-ṬEMUI.

Ȧat V. ȦATENKHU. The Spirits here live upon the inert and feeble. Its god was probably OSIRIS.

[1] Sheets 28, 29, and 30.

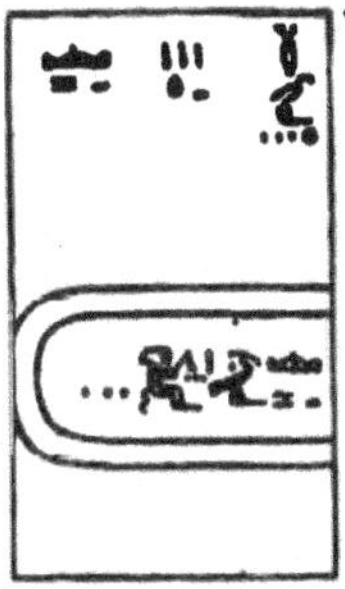

Åat III.

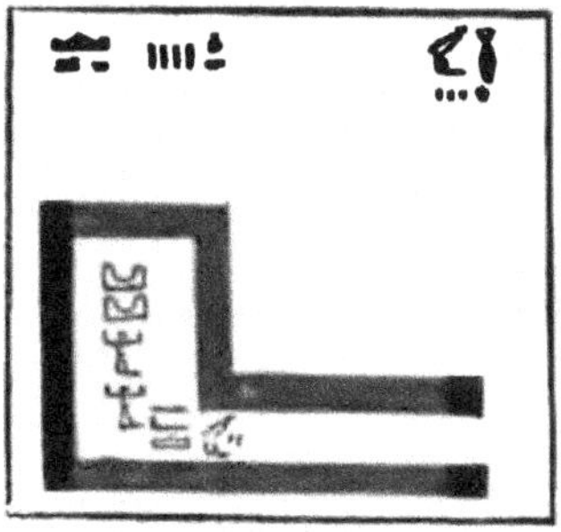

Åat IV.

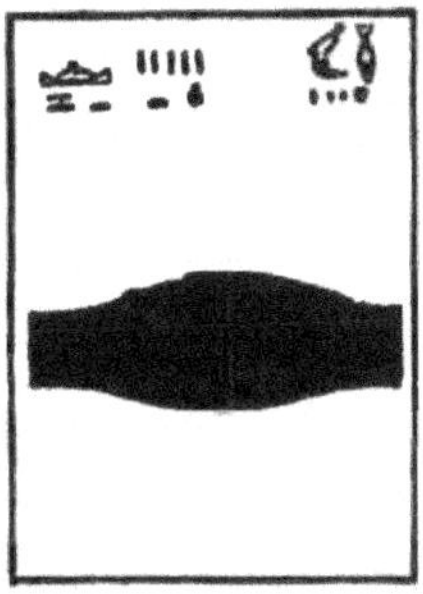

Åat V.

Åat VI. ÅMMEḤET, which is presided over either by SEKHER-ĀṬ or SEKHER-REMUS. This Åat was sacred to the gods, the Spirits could not find it out, and it was accursed for the dead.

Åat VII. ÅSES, a region of burning, fiery flame, wherein the serpent REREK lives.

Åat VIII. HA-ḤETEP, a region containing roaring torrents of water, and ruled over by a god called QA-HA-ḤETEP. A variant gives the name of this Åat as HA-SERT, and that of its god as FA-PET.

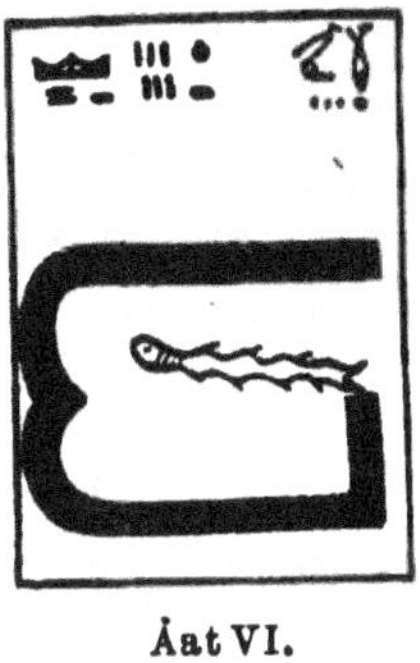

Åat VI.

Åat VII.

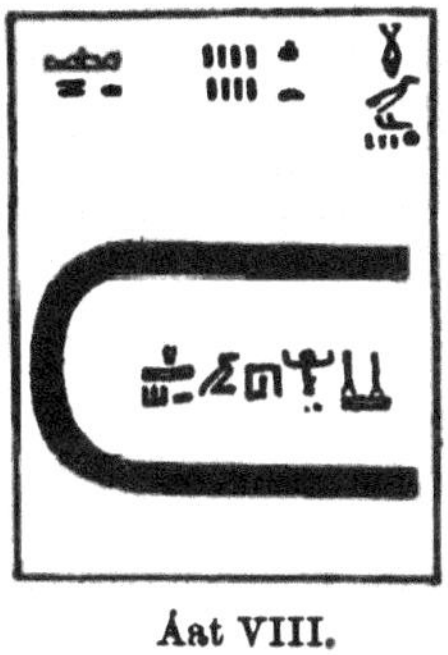

Åat VIII.

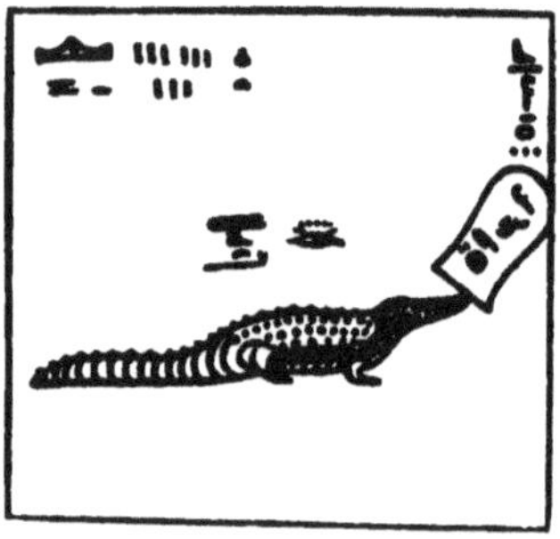
Åat IX.

Åat X.

Åat IX. ÅKESI, a region which is unknown even to the gods; its god was MAA-THETEF, and its only inhabitant is the "god who dwelleth in his egg."

Åat X. NUT-ENT-QAḤU, i.e., the city of Qaḥu. It was also known by the name ÅPT-ENT-QAḤU. The gods of this region appear to have been NĀU, KAPET, and NEḤEB-KAU.

Åat XI. ÅṬU, the god of which was SEPṬ (Sothis).

Åat XII. UNT, the god of which was ḤETEMET-BAIU; also called ÅSTCHEṬET-EM-ÅMENT.

Åat XI.

Åat XII.

Åat XIII. UĀRT-ENT-MU: its deity was the hippopotamus-god called HEBṬ-RE-F.

Åat XIV. The mountainous region of KHER-ĀḤA, the god of which was ḤĀP, the Nile.

A brief examination of this list of Åats, or Regions, suggests that the divisions of Sekhet-ḥetepet given in it are arranged in order from south to north, for it is well known that Åmentet, the first Åat, was entered from the neighbourhood of Thebes, and that the last-mentioned Åat, i.e., Kher-āḥa, represents a region quite

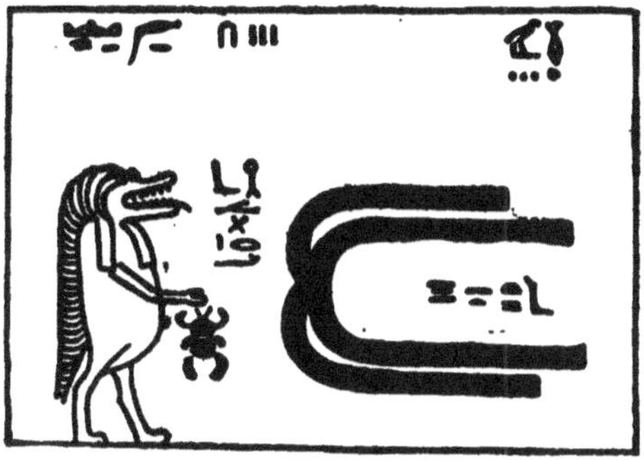

Åat XIII.

Åat XIV.

close to Heliopolis; if this be so, Sekhet-Åaru was probably situated at no great distance from Abydos, near which was the famous "Gap" in the mountains, whereby the spirits of the dead entered the abode set apart for them. We see from this list also that the heaven provided for the blessed was one such as an agricultural population would expect to have, and a nation of farmers would revel in the idea of living among fields of wheat and barley, the former being between seven and eight feet, and the latter between nine and ten feet high. The spirits who reaped this grain are said to have been nine cubits, i.e., over thirteen feet, in height, a statement which seems to indicate that a belief in the existence of men of exceptional height in very ancient days was extant in Egypt traditionally.

Other facts to be gleaned from the list of Åats concerning Sekhet-Åaru are that:—1. One section at least was filled with fire. 2. Another was filled with rushing, roaring waters, which swept everything away before them. 3. In another the serpent Rerek lived. 4. In another the Spirits lived upon the inert and the feeble. 5. In another lived the "Destroyer of Souls." 6. The great antiquity of the ideas about the Åats is proved by the appearance of the names of Ḥāp, the Nile-god, Sepṭ, or Sothis, and the Hippopotamus-goddess, Hebṭ-re-f, in connection with them.

The qualification for entering the Åats was not so much the living of a good life upon earth as a knowledge of the magical figures which represented them, and their names; these are given twice in the Papyrus of Nu, and as they are of great importance for the study of magical pictures they have been reproduced above.

Of the general form and the divisions of Sekhet-Åaru, or the "Field of Reeds," and Sekhet-ḥetepet, or the "Field of Peace," thanks to the funeral papyri of the XVIIIth Dynasty, much is known, and they may now be briefly described. From the Papyrus of Nebseni [1] we learn that Sekhet-ḥetep was rectangular in shape, and that it was intersected by canals, supplied from the stream by which the whole region was enclosed. In one division were three pools of water,

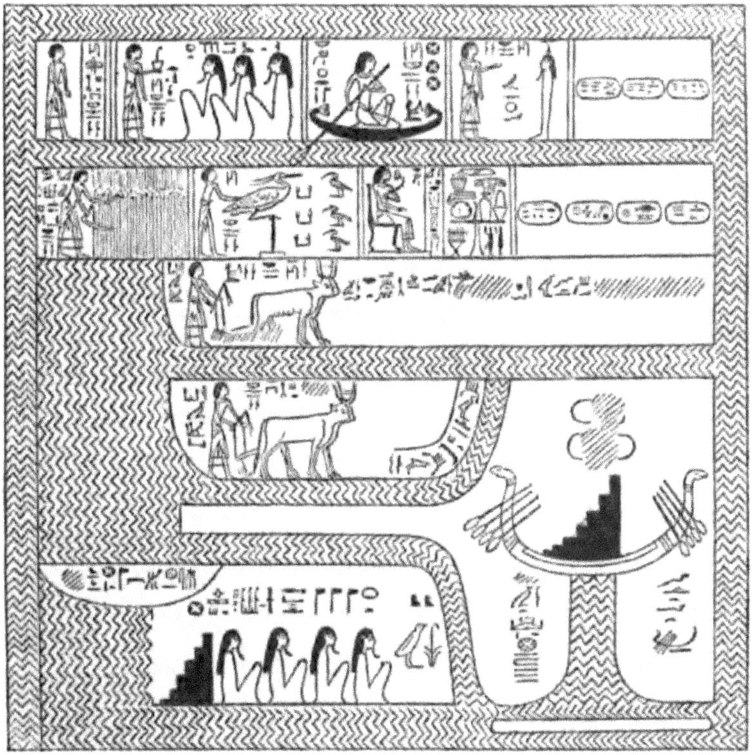

Sekhet-Ḥetepet (Papyrus of Nebseni, British Museum, No. 9900, sheet 17).

in another four pools, and in a third two pools; a place specially set apart was known as the "birthplace of the god of the region," and the "great company of the

[1] British Museum, No. 9,900, sheet 17.

gods in Sekhet-ḥetep" occupied another section of it. At the end of a short canal was moored a boat, provided with eight oars or paddles, and each end of it terminated in a serpent's head; in it was a flight of steps. The deceased, as we see, also possessed a boat wherein he sailed about at will, but its form is different from that of the boat moored at the end of the canal. The operations of ploughing, and of seed-time and harvest, are all represented. As to the deceased himself, we see him in the act of offering incense to the "great company of the gods," and he addresses a bearded figure, which is intended probably to represent his father, or some near relation; we see him paddling in a boat, and also sitting on a chair of state smelling a flower, with a table of offerings before him. None of the inscriptions mentions Sekhet-Åaru, but it is distinctly said that the reaping of the grain by the deceased is taking place in Sekhet-ḳetep, 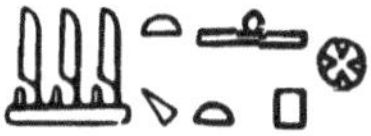, or Sekhet-ḥetepet, 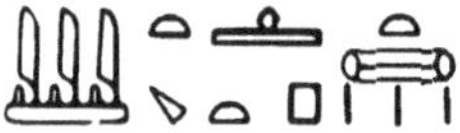.

In chronological order the next picture of Sekhet-ḥetepet to be considered is that from the Papyrus of Ani, and it will be seen at a glance that in details it differs from that already described. Ani adores the gods in the first division, but he burns no incense; the boat in which he paddles is loaded with offerings, and he is seen dedicating an offering to the bearded figure. The legend reads, "Living in peace in Sekhet—winds for the nostrils." The second division contains scenes

Sekhet-Ḥetepet (Papyrus of Ani, British Museum, No. 10,470, sheet 32).

of reaping and treading out of corn, but only three pools of water instead of four. In the third division we see Ani ploughing the land by the side of a stream of untold length and breadth, which is said to contain neither fish nor worms. It is important to note that this division is described as SEKHET-ÅANRU, . The eyot which represents the birthplace of the god of the city has no title, and the larger island, which is separated from it by a very narrow strip of ground, contains a flight of steps, but no gods. In the left-hand corner is a place which is described as "the seat of the Spirits, who are seven cubits in height"; the "grain is three cubits high, and it is the perfect Spirits who reap it." In the other portion of this section are two boats instead of one as in the Papyrus of Nebseni.

In connection with the two pictures of Sekhet-ḥetepet described above, it is important to consider the text which accompanies the older of them, i.e., that of the Papyrus of Nebseni. The deceased is made to say that he sails over the Lake of Ḥetep (i.e., Peace) in a boat which he brought from the house of Shu, and that he has come to the city of Ḥetep under the favour of the god of the region, who is also called Ḥetep. He says, "My mouth is strong, I am equipped [with words "of power to use as weapons] against the Spirits "let them not have dominion over me. Let me be "rewarded with thy fields, O thou god Ḥetep. That "which is thy wish do, O lord of the winds. May I "become a spirit therein, may I eat therein, may I "drink therein, may I plough therein, may I reap "therein, may I fight therein, may I make love therein, "may my words be powerful therein, may I never be "in a state of servitude therein, and may I be in "authority therein. . . . . . [Let me] live with the "god Ḥetep, clothed, and not despoiled by the 'lords "of the north,'[1] and may the lords of divine things "bring food unto me. May he make me to go forward "and may I come forth; may he bring my power to "me there, may I receive it, and may my equipment "be from the god Ḥetep. May I gain dominion over "the great and mighty word which is in my body in "this my place, and by it I shall have memory and "not forget." The pools and places in Sekhet-ḥetepet which the deceased mentions as having a desire to visit are UNEN-EM-ḤETEP, the first large division of the region; NEBT-TAUI, a pool in the second division; NUT-URT, a pool in the first division; UAKH, a pool in the second division, where the *kau*, or "doubles," dwell; TCHEFET, a portion of the third division, wherein the deceased arrays himself in the apparel of Rā; UNEN-EM-ḤETEP, the birthplace of the Great God; QENQENTET, a pool in the first division, where he sees his father, and

[1] Probably the marauding seamen who traded on the coasts of the Mediterranean, and who sometimes landed and pillaged the region near which the primitive Elysian Fields were supposed to have been situated.

looks upon his mother, and has intercourse with his wife, and where he catches worms and serpents and frees himself from them; the Lake of TCHESERT, wherein he plunges, and so cleanses himself from all impurities; ḤAST, where the god ÅRI-EN-ÅB-F binds on his head for him; USERT, a pool in the first division, and SMAM, a pool in the third division of Sekhet-ḥetepet. Having visited all these places, and recited all the words of power with which he was provided, and ascribed praises to the gods, the deceased brings his boat to anchor, and, presumably, takes up his abode in the Field of Peace for ever.

From the extract from the Chapter of Sekhet-Åaru and Sekhet-ḥetepet given above, it is quite clear that the followers of Osiris hoped and expected to do in the next world exactly what they had done in this, and that they believed they would obtain and continue to live their life in the world to come by means of a word of power; and that they prayed to the god Ḥetep for dominion over it, so that they might keep it firmly in their memories, and not forget it. This is another proof that in the earliest times men relied in their hope of a future life more on the learning and remembering of a potent name or formula than on the merits of their moral and religious excellences. From first to last throughout the chapter there is no mention of the god Osiris, unless he be the "Great God" whose birthplace is said to be in the region Unen-em-ḥetep, and nowhere in it is there any suggestion that the permission or favour of Osiris is necessary for those who would enter either Sekhet-Åaru or Sekhet-ḳetep. This seems to indicate that the conceptions about the Other World, at least so far as the "realms of the blest" were concerned, were evolved in the minds of Egyptian theologians before Osiris attained to the high position which he occupied in the Dynastic Period. On the other hand, the evidence on this point which is to be deduced from the Papyrus of Ani must be taken into account.

At the beginning of this Papyrus we have first of all Hymns to Rā and Osiris, and the famous Judgment Scene which is familiar to all. We see the heart of Ani being weighed in the Balance against the symbol of righteousness in the presence of the Great Company of the Gods, and the weighing takes place at one end of the house of Osiris, whilst Osiris sits in his shrine at the other. The "guardian of the Balance" is Anubis, and the registrar is Thoth, the scribe of the gods, who is seen noting the result of the weighing. In the picture the beam of the Balance is quite level, which shows that the heart of Ani exactly counterbalances the symbol of righteousness. This result Thoth announces to the gods in the following words, "In very truth the heart of Osiris hath been weighed, "and his soul hath stood as a witness for him; its case "is right (i.e., it hath been found true by trial) in the "Great Balance. No wickedness hath been found in "him, he hath not purloined the offerings in the "temples,[1] and he hath done no evil by deed or word "whilst he was upon earth." The gods in their reply accept Thoth's report, and declare that, so far as they are concerned, Ani has committed neither sin nor evil. Further, they go on to say that he shall not be delivered over to the monster Āmemet, and they order that he shall have offerings, that he shall have the power to go into the presence of Osiris, and that he shall have a homestead, or allotment, in Sekhet-ḥetepet for ever. We next see Ani being led into the presence of Osiris by Horus, the son of Isis, who reports that the heart of Ani hath sinned against no god or goddess; as it hath also been found just and righteous according to the written laws of the gods, he asks that Ani may have cakes and ale given to him, and the power to appear before Osiris, and that he may take his place among the "Followers of Horus," and be like them for ever.

Now from this evidence it is clear that Ani was considered to have merited his reward in Sekhet-ḥetepet by the righteousness and integrity of his life upon earth as regards his fellow-man, and by the reverence and worship which he paid to every god and every goddess; in other words, it is made to appear that he had earned his reward, or had justified himself by his works. Because his heart had emerged

[1] Ani was the receiver of the ecclesiastical revenues of the gods of Thebes and Abydos, and the meaning here is that he did not divert to his own use any portion of the goods he received.

triumphantly from its trial the gods decreed for him the right to appear in the presence of the god Osiris, and ordered him to be provided with a homestead in Sekhet-ḥetep. There is no mention of any repentance on Ani's part for wrong done; indeed, he says definitely, "There is no sin in my body. I have not "uttered wittingly that which is untrue, and I have "committed no act having a double motive [in my "mind]." As he was troubled by no remembrance of sin, his conscience was clear, and he expected to receive his reward, not as an act of mercy on the part of the gods, but as an act of justice. Thus it would seem that repentance played no part in the religion of the primitive inhabitants of Egypt, and that a man atoned for his misdeeds by the giving of offerings, by sacrifice, and by worship. On the other hand, Nebseni is made to say to the god of Sekhet-ḥetep, "Let me be rewarded "with thy fields, O Ḥetep; but do thou according to "thy will, O lord of the winds." This petition reveals a frame of mind which recognizes submissively the omnipotence of the god's will, and the words "do thou according to thy will" are no doubt the equivalent of those which men of all nations and in every age have prayed—"Thy will be done."

The descriptions of the pictures of Sekhet-ḥetep given above make it evident that the views expressed in the Papyrus of Nebseni differ in some important details from those which we find in the Papyrus of Ani, but whether this difference is due to some general

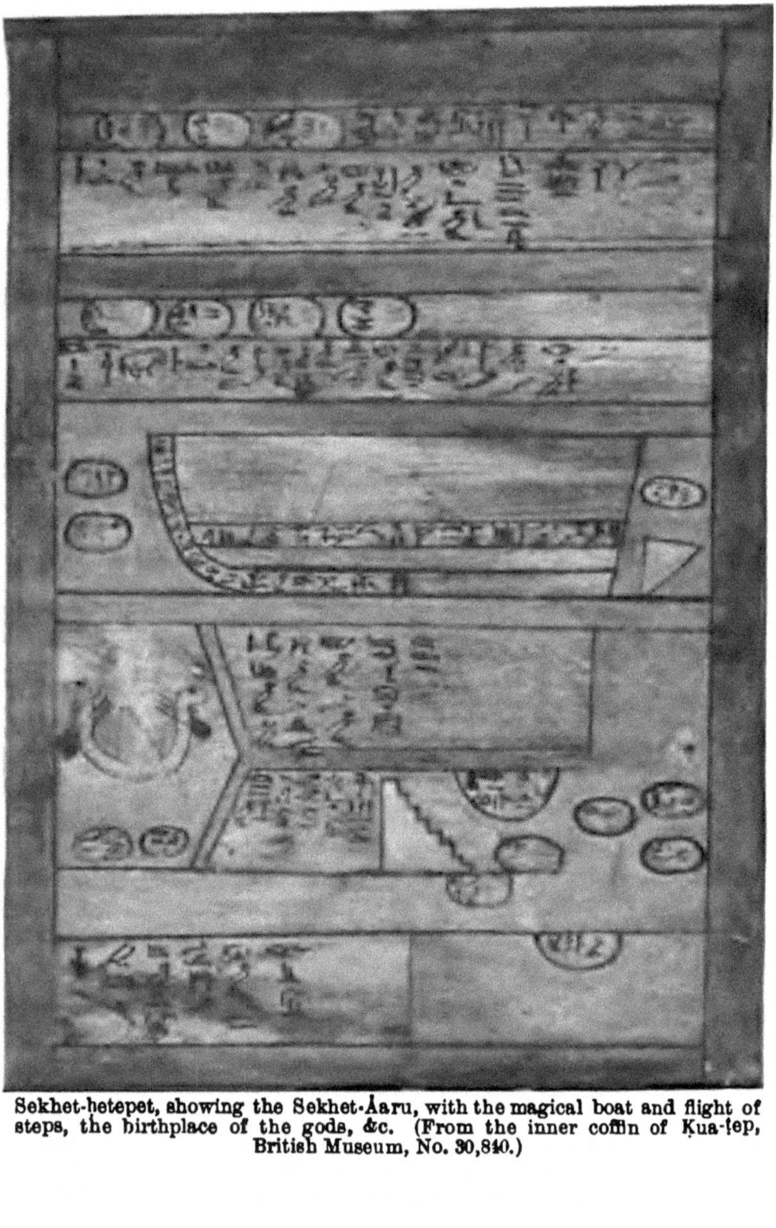

Sekhet-ḥetepet, showing the Sekhet-Åaru, with the magical boat and flight of steps, the birthplace of the gods, &c. (From the inner coffin of Ḳua-ṭep, British Museum, No. 30,840.)

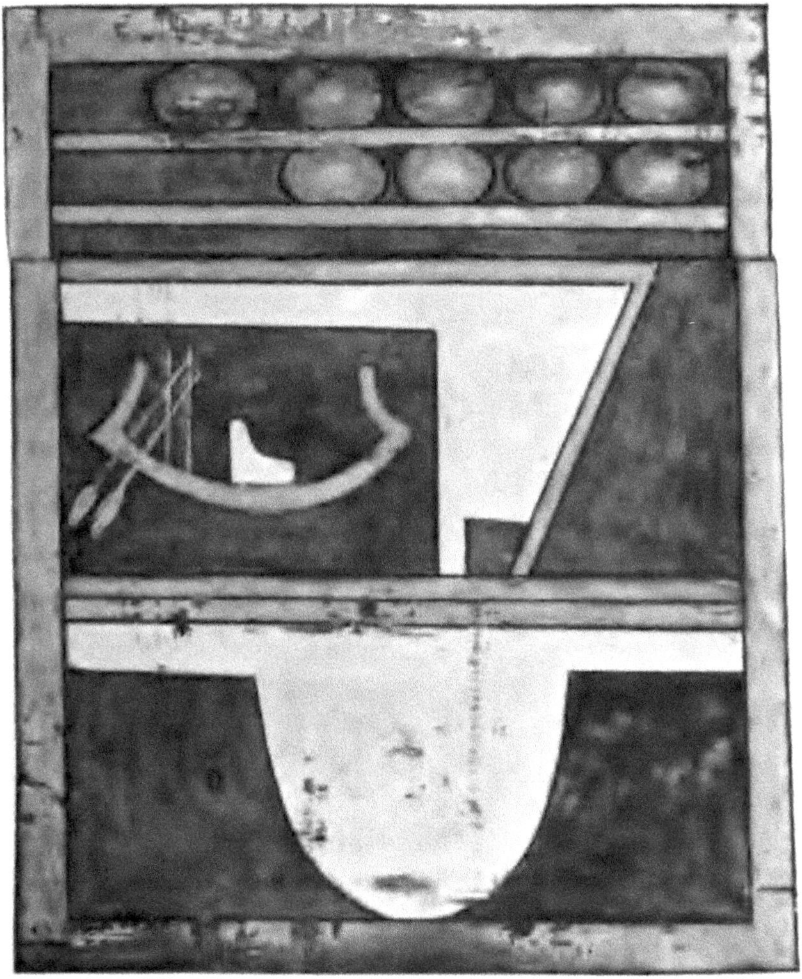

Sekhet-ḥetepet, showing the Sekhet-Aaru, with the magical boat, the nine lakes, the birthplace of the gods, &c. (From the outer coffin of Sen, British Museum, No. 30,841.)

development in religious thought, which took place in the interval between the periods when the papyri were written, cannot be said. There is abundant evidence in the Papyrus of Ani that Ani himself was a very religious man, and we are not assuming too much when we say that he was the type of a devout worshipper of Osiris, whose beliefs, though in some respects of a highly spiritual character, were influenced by the magic and gross material views which seem to have been inseparable from the religion of every Egyptian. Though intensely logical in some of their views about the Other World, the Egyptians were very illogical in others, and they appear to have seen neither difficulty nor absurdity in holding at the same time beliefs which were inconsistent and contradictory. It must, however, in fairness be said that this characteristic was due partly to their innate conservatism in religious matters, and their respect for the written word, and partly to their fear that they might prejudice their interests in the future life if they rejected any scripture or picture which antiquity, or religious custom, or tradition had sanctioned.

Certain examples, however, prove that the Egyptians of one period were not afraid to modify or develop ideas which had come down to them from another, as may be seen from the accompanying illustration. The picture which is reproduced on p. 54 is intended to represent Sekhet-ḥetepet, and is taken from the inner coffin of Ḳua-Ṭep, which was found at Al-Barsha, and is now in the British Museum (No. 30,840); it dates from the period of the XIth Dynasty. From this we see that the country of the blessed was rectangular in shape, and surrounded by water, and intersected by streams, and that, in addition to large tracts of land, there were numbers of eyots belonging to it. In many pictures these eyots are confounded with lakes, but it is pretty clear that the "Islands of the Blessed" were either fertile eyots, or oases which appeared to be green islands in a sea of sand. Near the first section were three, near the second four, near the third four, three being oval, and one triangular; the fourth section was divided into three parts by means of a canal with two arms, and contained the birthplace of the god, and near it were seven eyots; the fifth is the smallest division of all, and has only one eyot near it. Each eyot has a name which accorded with its chief characteristic; the dimensions of three of the streams or divisions are given, the region where ploughing takes place is indicated, and the positions of the staircase and the mystic boat are clearly shown. The name of the god Ḥetep occurs twice, and that of Osiris once.

If now we compare this picture with that from the Papyrus of Nebseni we shall find that the actual operations of ploughing, reaping, and treading out of the corn are depicted on the Papyrus, and that several figures of gods and the deceased have been added. The text speaks of offerings made by the deceased, and of his sailing in a boat, &c., therefore the artist

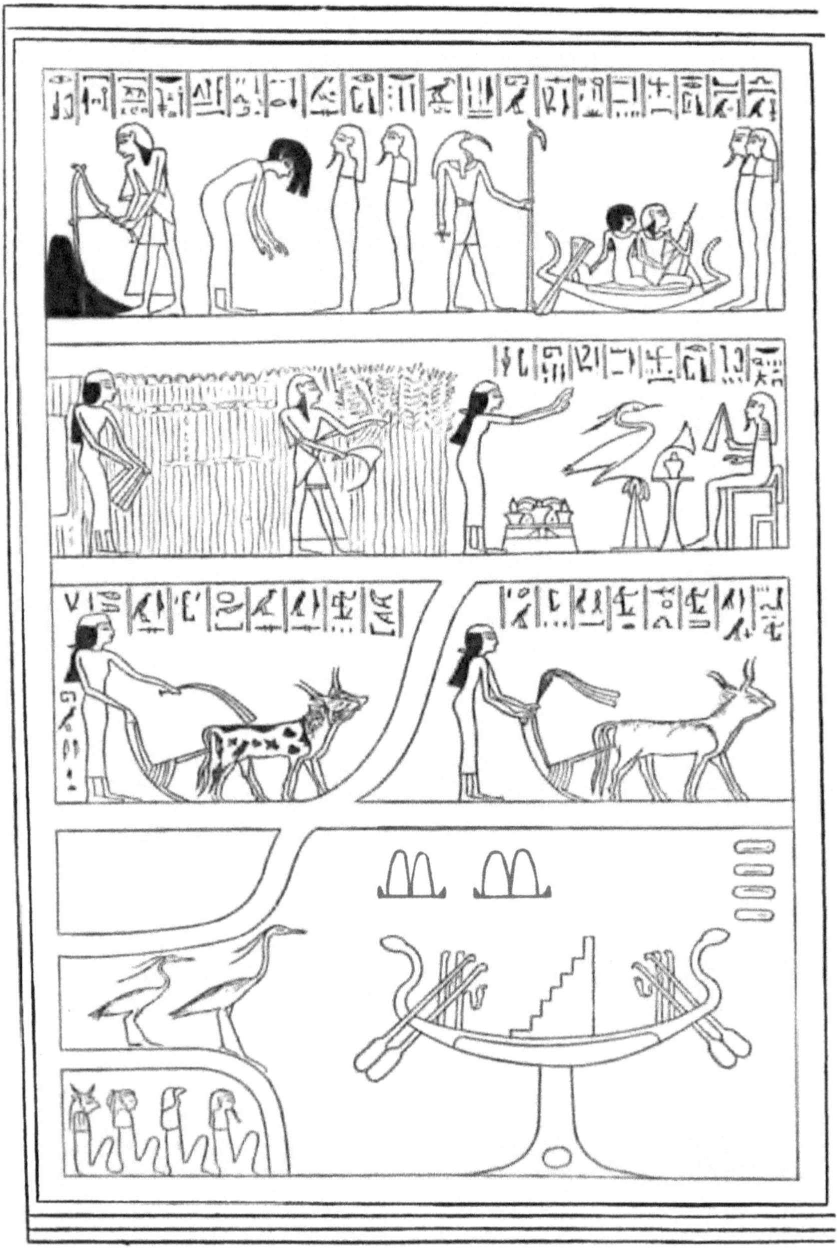

Sekhet-ḥetepet. (From the Papyrus of Ánhai—XXIInd Dynasty.)

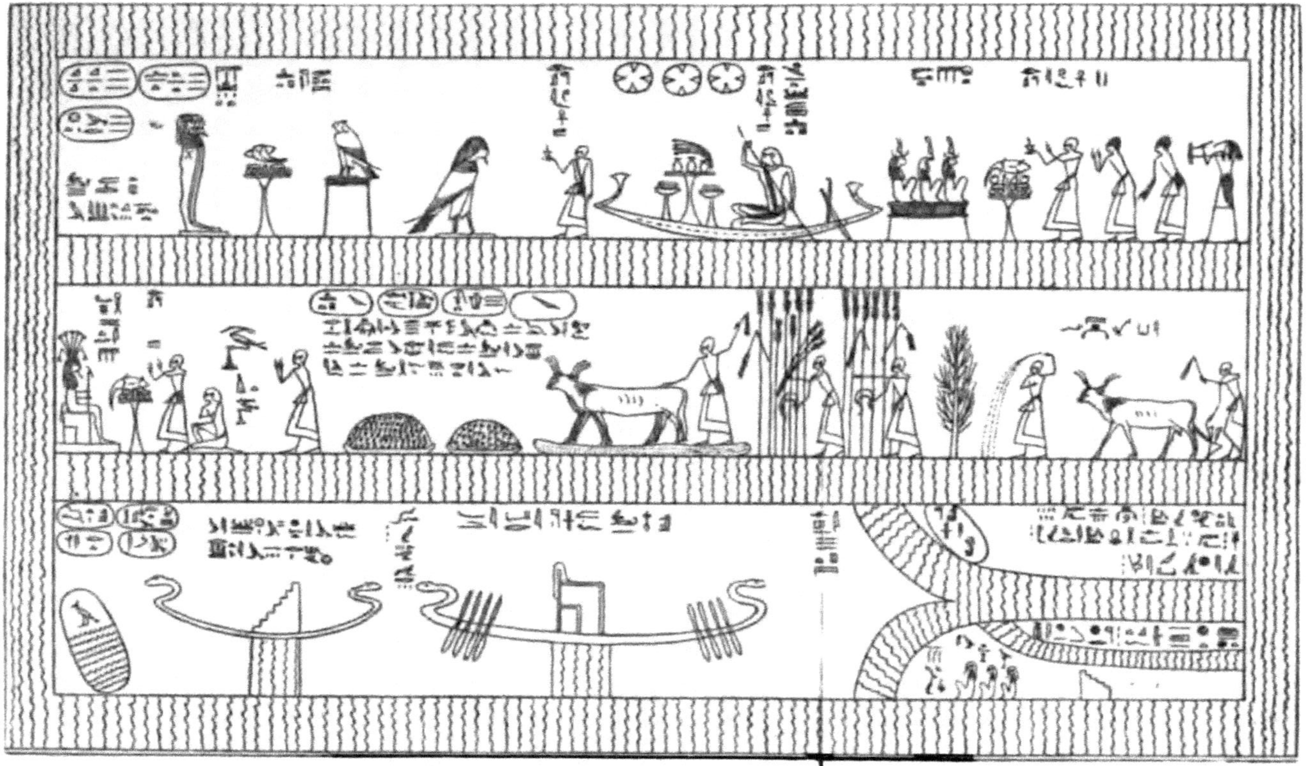

Sekhet-ḥetepet. (From the Turin Papyrus—Ptolemaïc Period.)

added scenes in which he is depicted doing these things; and the lower part of the picture in the Papyrus has been modified considerably. In the second division it may be noted that Nebseni is seen laying both hands on the back of the Bennu bird; there is no authority for this in the older copy of the picture. In the illustration on p. 55, which is reproduced from the coffin of Sen, in the British Museum (No. 30,841), a still simpler form of Sekhet-ḥetepet is seen; here we have only nine eyots, which are grouped together, and no inscription of any kind.

Still further modifications were introduced into the pictures of Sekhet-ḥetepet drawn in later times, and, in order that the reader may be enabled to trace some of the most striking of these, copies of Sekhet-ḥetepet from the Papyrus of Ȧnhai (about B.C. 1040), and from that of Ȧuf-ānkh (Ptolemaïc Period), are reproduced on pp. 60 and 61.

CHAPTER III.

THE REUNION OF THE BEATIFIED AND THEIR RECOGNITION OF EACH OTHER IN THE OTHER WORLD.

HAVING now described Sekhet-ḥetep and the Halls and Gates of the Other World according to the Book of Coming Forth by Day (PER-EM-HRU), we may pass on to consider how far souls in Sekhet-ḥetep had the power to know and recognize each other, and to enjoy intercourse with relatives and friends. From many scenes and passages in texts it has for some time past been clear that husband met wife, and wife met husband again beyond the grave, for in the Papyrus of Ani we see Ani accompanied by his wife in the House of Osiris and in many other places, and in the Papyrus of Ȧnhai [1] we see Anhai bowing before two mummied forms, which represent her father and mother, and seated in a boat side by side with her husband. From the Papyrus of Nebseni [2] we know that the meeting of the deceased with his mother, father, and wife was believed to take place on the island in the first division of Sekhet-ḥetep called Qenqentet, for he says,

[1] See page 60.
[2] *Book of the Dead*, Chapter CX., line 39.

"O Qenqentet, I have entered into thee, and I have "seen the Osiris (*i.e.*, his father) and I have gazed "upon my mother, and had union [with my wife]."[1] Other passages in the PER-EM-HRU indicate that the Egyptian hoped to meet again other people besides his father, mother, and wife, in Sekhet-ḥetep. Thus in the LIInd Chapter the deceased is made to say, "Let me "have the power to manage my own fields in Ṭaṭṭu "(Mendes), and my own growing crops in Ȧnnu (Helio-"polis). Let me live upon bread made from white grain, "and let my beer be made from red grain, and may my "ancestors, and my father and my mother be given unto "me as guardians of my door and for the ordering of "my territory." This petition is repeated in Chapter CLXXXIX., lines 7-9, which was written with the object of preventing a man from being hungry, and so being obliged to eat filth or offal.

From another passage (Chapter LXVIII., lines 13, 14) it is clear that the deceased expected to find in the Other World slaves, or domestic servants, who would help him to cultivate the land which he believed would be allotted to him, and there is reason for supposing that such beings would have been known to him upon earth. He says, "I have gained the mastery over the

[1] 

From this passage it seems that a man who died before his wife expected to find another woman in Sekhet-ḥetep whom he might marry.

"waters, I have gained the mastery over the canal, I "have gained the mastery over the river, I have gained "the mastery over the furrows, I have gained the "mastery over the men who work for me, I have "gained the mastery over the women who work for "me in Neter-khert, I have gained the mastery over "the things which were decreed to me on earth in "Neter-khert." Thus we see that every pious Egyptian hoped to live again with the members of his household after death in Sekhet-ḥetepet.

Now the word which I have rendered "ancestors" in the extract given above is *abtu*, , or *abut*, and its form and evident meaning suggest a comparison with the common Semitic word for "fathers"; the determinatives  prove that the word describes people of both sexes. It occurs twice in the PER-EM-HRU, viz., in Chapter LII., line 6, and Chapter CLXXXIX., line 7,[1] and was translated "persons" by me in 1896; the oldest example of the use of the word was published by M. P. Lacau in *Recueil*, 1904, p. 67.

The very short form of the prayer of the deceased that he may enjoy the companionship of his father and mother in Sekhet-ḥetep is the outcome of a belief which is very ancient; and it finds its fullest expression in an

[1] See my edition of the *Chapters of Coming Forth by Day*, text, pp. 124, 493.

important Chapter, which M. Lacau has published[1] according to the texts on two coffins of the XIth Dynasty, which were found at Al-Barsha, and are now in the Egyptian Museum at Cairo.[2] This Chapter supplies us with some valuable information concerning the reunion and recognition of relatives and friends in Sekhet-ḥetep, and M. Lacau's excellent edition of the text is a useful contribution to the literature which specially concerns Sekhet-ḥetep. The words which stand at the head of the Chapter read, "THE GATHERING TOGETHER OF THE ANCESTORS OF A MAN TO HIM IN NETER KHER,"[3] and the text begins:

"Hail, Rā! Hail, Tem! Hail, Seb! Hail, Nut! Grant "ye unto Sepȧ that he may traverse the heavens (or "sky), that he may traverse the earth, that he may "traverse the waters, that he may meet his ancestors, "may meet his father, may meet his mother, may meet "his grown up sons and daughters, and his brethren, "and his sisters, may meet his friends, both male and "female, may meet those who have been as parents to "him,[4] and his kinsfolk (cousins ?),[5] and those who have "worked for him upon earth, both male and female, and "may meet the concubine whom he loved and knew."

[1] See RECUEIL, 1904, pp. 67-72, and *La Réunion de la Famille*, by M. J. Baillet, in *Journal Asiatique*, Xème Série, tom. iv., p. 307, where a rendering of the Chapter into French will be found.

[2] They bear the numbers 28083 and 28087.

[3] A name of the Underworld.

[4] Perhaps "his uncles and aunts," or "foster-parents."

[5] Or "connexions."

"Behold, O Qema-ur (i.e., Great Creator), make Sepȧ "to rejoin his grown up sons and daughters, and his "concubines whom it is his heart's desire [to meet], and "make thou Sepȧ to rejoin his friends, both male and "female, and those who have worked for him upon earth."

"And if it happen that his father should be turned "aside, or opposed or removed, when he would appear "to him, or his mother when she would reveal herself to "him, when Sepȧ wisheth to rejoin his ancestors, and "his father and his mother, and his men and his women, "and if it happen that there should be turned aside, "or opposed, or done away the reunion of Sepȧ with "his little children, or his reunion with his brethren "and sisters, and with his friends, and with his foster-"parents, and with his kinsfolk, and with those who "have worked for him upon earth: then verily the "heart which is provided [with words of power] shall "be removed from Rā, and the choice oxen for sacrifice "shall be driven away from the altars of the gods, "and the bread-cakes shall not be shattered, and the "white bread-cakes shall not be broken in pieces, the "meat-offering shall not be cut up in the divine "chamber of sacrifice, and for you ropes shall not "be coiled, and for you boats shall not be manned.

"But if he shall be with his father when he "appeareth, and if he shall receive his mother when "she maketh herself visible, and if he shall be "rejoined to his ancestors and to his fathers and his "mothers, and his men and his women, and his little "children, and his beloved ones, and his foster-parents, "and his kinsfolk, and his [grown-up] sons and "daughters, and his concubines, whom it is his heart's "desire [to meet], and his friends, and those who have "worked for him upon earth; and if he shall rejoin all "his ancestors in heaven, and on earth, and in Neter-"kher, and in the sky, and in Åakeb (i.e., a region of the "sky), and in Ḥāp (the Nile), and in Aḳeb (i.e. the "watery abyss of the sky), and in Ḥet-ur-kau, and in "Ṭeṭu, and in Ṭeṭet (?), and in Pa-ur, and in Āḥakher, "and in Ābṭu: then verily the bread-cakes shall be "shattered, and the white bread-cakes shall be broken "in pieces, and verily the meat offerings shall be cut up "in the divine chamber of sacrifice, and verily ropes "shall be coiled, and verily boats shall be manned, and "verily the Boat of Rā shall journey on its way, being "rowed by the mariners of the ÅKHEMU-SEKU and the "ÅKHEMU-URTCHU; now his name is unknown, his "name is unknown.

"The goddess Hathor surroundeth Sepå with the "magical protection of life, but it is Seb who equippeth "him.[1] The sister of Sepå [and] wife [is] the guardian "of the wood of the Great Field.[2] And, moreover,

[1] Or, It is Seb who is the funeral chest, or sarcophagus, the allusion being to the fact that it was in the body of Seb, i.e., the earth, that the deceased was laid.

[2] The meaning of this line is not clear to me. The word *khet* , is often applied to wheat or barley, as the "wood," or "plant" of life. By "Great Field" I understand Sekhet-ḥetep.

"the sister of Sepȧ, the guardian of the wood of the "Great Field, saith, 'Verily thou shalt come with "rejoicing, and thy heart shall be glad, and there shall "be food to Sepȧ, and winds shall be given unto thee, "yea, thy ancestors have commanded this [to be done]'; "therefore shall Sepȧ come with gladness, and his heart "shall be glad, and his ancestors shall be given unto "him. And the great ones of the ancestors of Sepȧ "shall come [to meet him] with joy, and their hearts "shall be glad when they meet him; and they shall "bear in their hands their staves, and their mattocks, "and their tools for ploughing, and their metal (?) "weapons of the earth, and shall deliver him from the "things which the goddess . . . . . . doeth, and from "the actions (?) of Nut, and from the mighty things "which the Two-Lion[1] God doeth to every soul, and "to every god. The ancestors of Sepȧ shall make him "to be delivered . . . . . [Rubric]. May be rejoined "ancestors, and father, and mother, and foster-parents, "and kinsfolk, and young children, and wives, and "concubines, and beloved ones (i.e., friends) male and "female, and servants (i.e., slaves), and the property "of every kind which belongeth to a man, to him in "Neter-kher (the Underworld)."

The Rubric ends with the words, "rope of Maāt, millions of times," which indicate that the whole Chapter, probably including the Rubric, was to be said by the person who wished to rejoin his friends in the

[1] I.e., Shu and Tefnut.

Underworld regularly and unceasingly for millions of times. The phrases *shes maāt ḥeḥ en sep* occur very often in the Theban Recension of the Book of the Dead, and a full list of the passages will be found in the *Vocabulary* to my edition of that work, page 328.

A perusal of the above Chapter shows that it is the expression of beliefs and ideas concerning the future life which belong to a very early period of civilization, and to a time when the Egyptians held most primitive views about their gods. The first paragraph calls upon two forms of the Sun-god, and the god of the earth, and the god of the sky, to allow the deceased to pass through the sky, and the earth, and the waters, to meet his ancestors, mother, father, wives, women of pleasure, sons and daughters of all ages, brothers and sisters, foster-parents (or perhaps uncles and aunts), cousins, connexions, friends of both sexes, "the doers of things," both men and women, etc. Portions of the second paragraph are difficult to render exactly, but it seems that in it the deceased is made to say that in the event of his being prevented from meeting or rejoining his father, mother, and other near and dear relatives and friends, the customary funeral offerings shall be promptly discontinued, and the heart of Rā, which is equipped with its word (of power), shall be removed from him; if, on the other hand, he is made to rejoin all his near and dear relatives and connexions, and is allowed and enabled to travel about and visit them in the various holy cities in heaven, bread and meat offerings shall be duly made on earth for the gods, and the Boat of Rā shall travel on its way. In other words, the deceased undertakes to provide offerings to the gods whom he mentions so long as he is allowed to rejoin his relatives at will, but if he is hindered in any way, he threatens that the progress of Rā himself shall be hindered, and that the god shall suffer the loss of his heart with its word of power.

The Cow-goddess Hathor is said to endue him with the protection of her magical power, and the earth-god Seb to supply him with all he needs, and the guardian of the staff [of life] promises that he shall be supplied with food and air in the Great Field, because the ancestors of the deceased who are already living there have given orders to this effect. These same ancestors, it is declared, shall come out to meet him, and as it is possible that some attempt may be made to stop or injure him by Seb (?), Nut, Shu and Tefnut, they shall bring their sticks, and staves, and clubs, and other weapons in their hands, so that they may be ready to defend their relative, and lead him to their abode. Here we have a good description of the manner in which Egyptian peasants have always turned out to defend a friend, and how they have always armed themselves with clubs, and sticks, and handles of ploughs, or flails, whenever a fellow villager had to be rescued from the clutches of foes or from the authorities, and have gone forth to his assistance. Not only would their spirits defend their spirit relative in the Other-

World, but they would also defend him by exactly the same means which their bodies would have employed to defend his body upon earth.

From one end of the chapter to the other there is no mention of Osiris, who in later times became the god of the Resurrection, and it is quite clear that the deceased believed that his reunion with his ancestors and family could be brought about without the help of any god, simply by the recital of the Chapter "Millions of times with never-ending regularity." The repetition of the whole chapter was unnecessary, for if a man recited the words of the Rubric an infinite number of times he would not only be able to rejoin his relatives, but also to regain in the Other World possession of all the property of every kind which he had enjoyed on this earth. The Rubric had, in fact, so far back as B.C. 2600, become a traditional magical formula of a most powerful character, and it must have been composed at the time when the abode of the blessed was supposed to resemble the "great field" in which the men of a village assembled to celebrate a festival, and before the ideas concerning Sekhet-Åaru and Sekhet-ḥetep, with which we are familiar from the "Book of Coming Forth by Day," were evolved. The texts of the Chapter and Rubric are of such interest that copies of them are printed as an Appendix to the present section.

We have now before us all the principal facts which are necessary for forming an opinion as to the kind of heaven which the primitive Egyptian hoped and expected to enjoy, and of the means which he took to obtain admission therein. He either bought, or persuaded, or forced, the "servant of the god," or priest, to give him words of power, i.e., names of gods, and magical formulae, which he learned, or had written down for him, and he relied for admission into the next world upon his knowledge of these, or copies of them which were buried with him, and upon the recitals of them at proper times and seasons by his relatives and friends, and upon offerings made upon earth to the gods on his behalf. Once in the abode of the blessed he was free to go wherever he pleased, to travel from one sacred place to another, to visit his friends, to eat, to drink, to enjoy the society of his wives and women of pleasure, and to rejoice in a family life which was only a glorified duplicate of that which he had known on earth. The gods he knew there were much like himself, and the extent and fervour of the worship which he devoted to them was exactly in proportion to the assistance which they rendered to him; his chief anxiety was not to forget the words of power which he had learned. His occupation consisted in watching the growth of crops, for all the necessary work was performed by beings who carried out his every behest. We now pass on to describe the abode of the blessed according to the "Book Åm-Ṭuat" and the "Book of Gates."

APPENDIX TO CHAPTER III.

THE CHAPTER OF THE GATHERING TOGETHER OF A MAN'S ANCESTORS TO HIM IN NETERKHER.

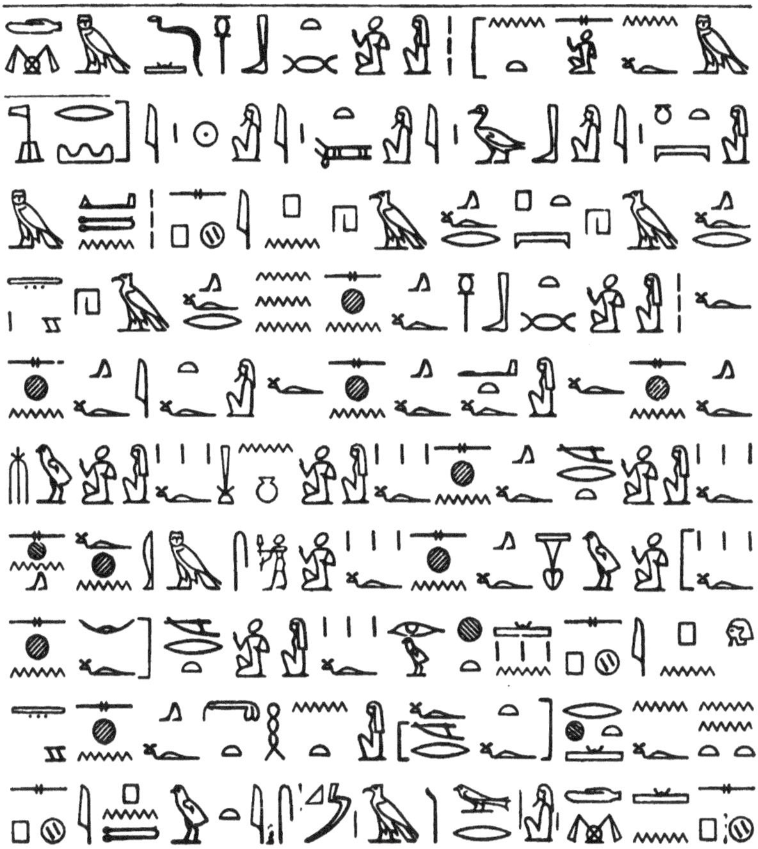

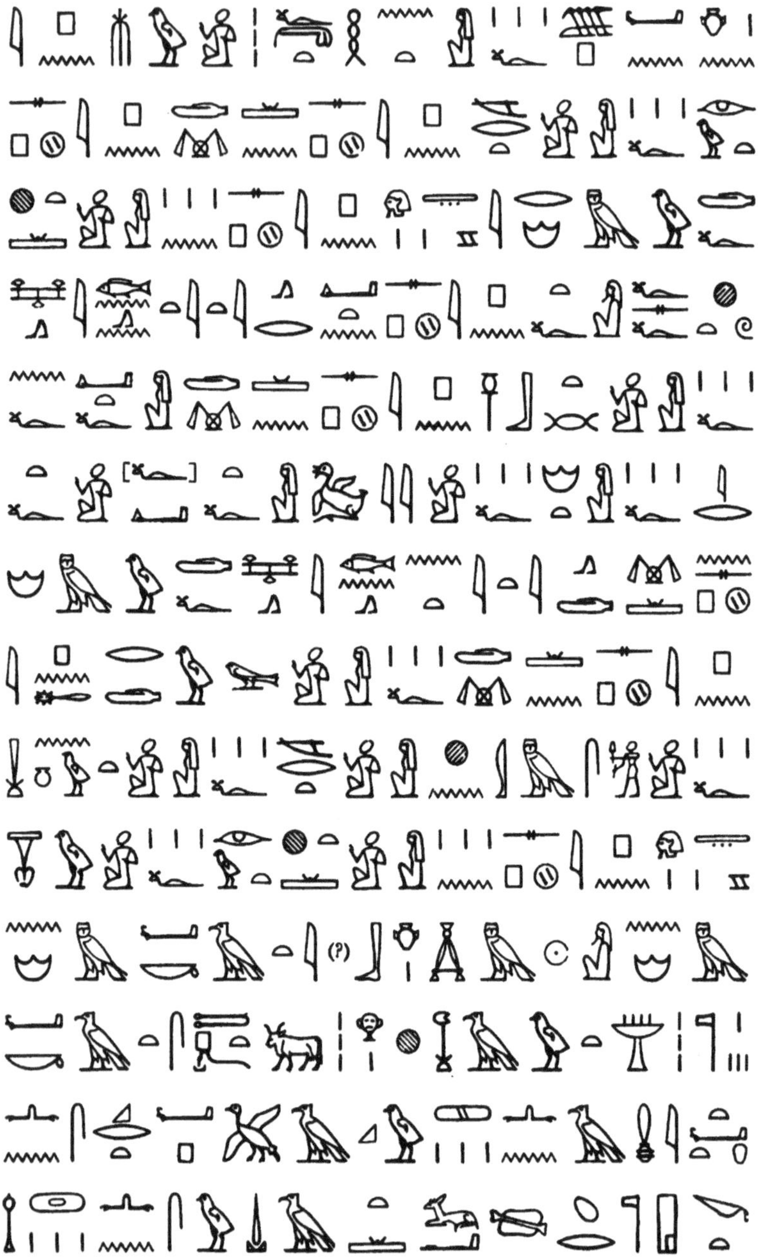

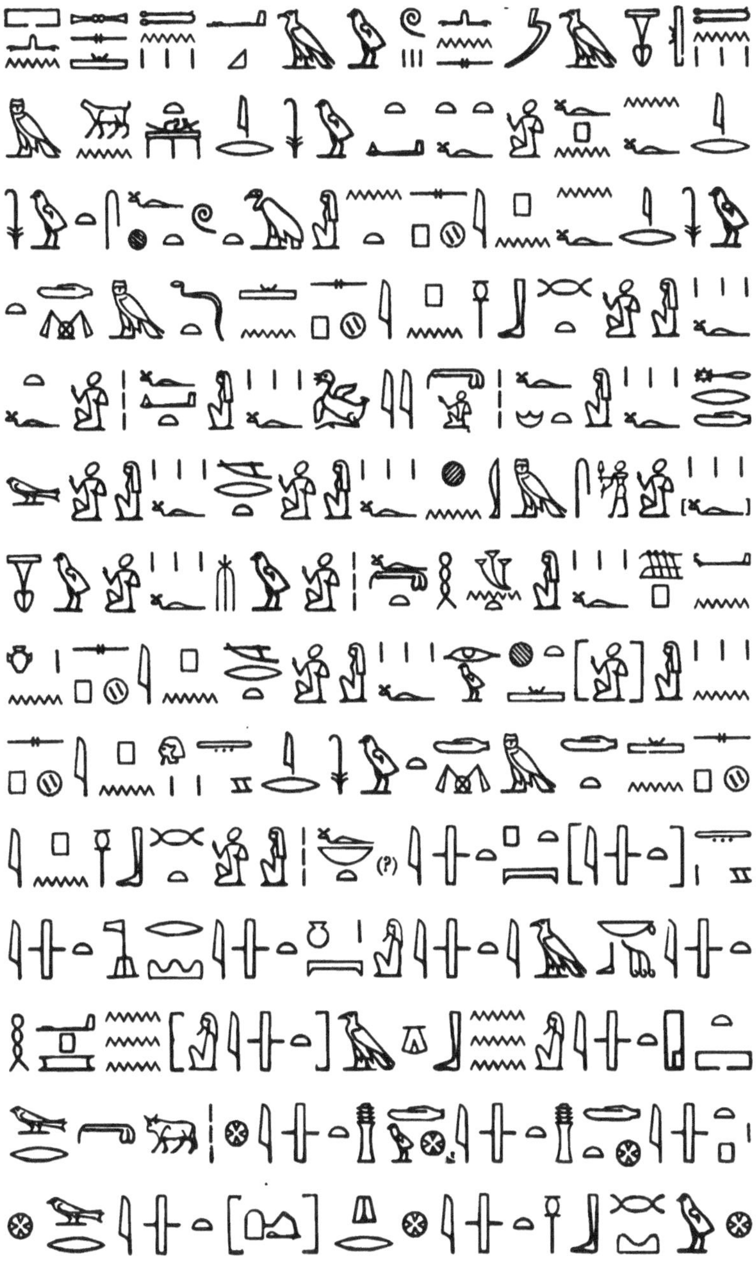

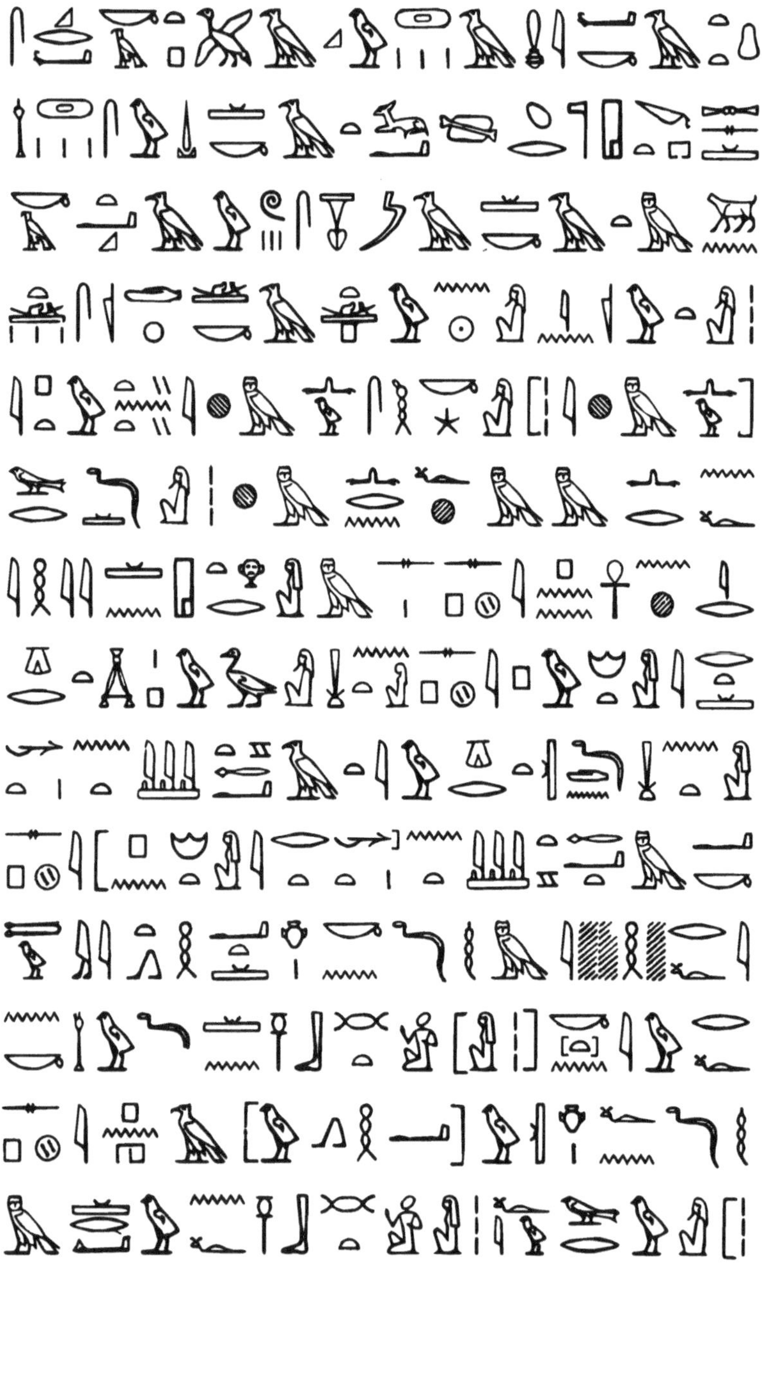

RUBRIC: 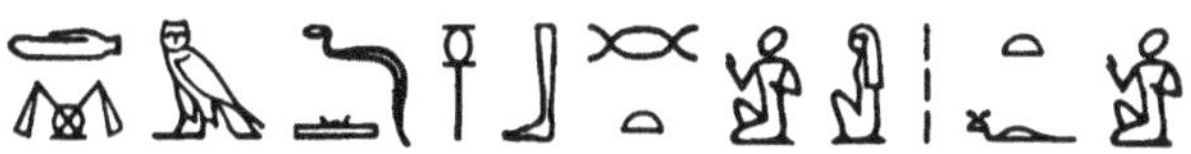

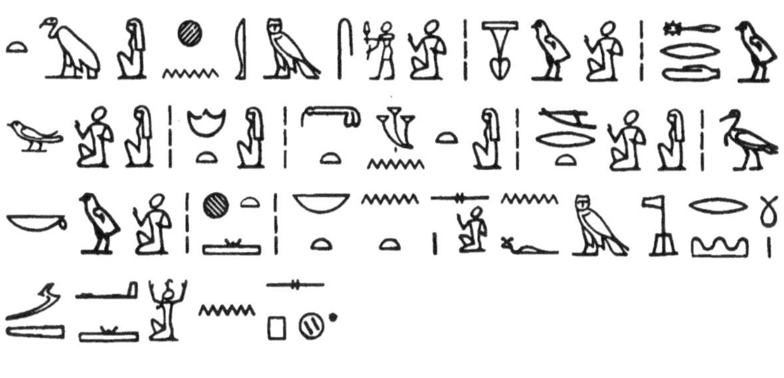

CHAPTER IV.

THE BOOK ȦM-ṬUAT AND THE BOOK OF GATES.

"ȦM-ṬUAT," or SHĀT ȦM-ṬUAT, i.e., the "Book of what is in the Ṭuat," is the name given by the Egyptians to the large funeral book in which the priests of Ȧmen describe the Other World according to the views of their order, and the passage of their god Ȧmen-Rā through the mysterious country which he traversed during the hours of the night. Its object, in the first place, was to impress the followers of Ȧmen and others with the idea of the absolute supremacy of that god in the realms of the dead, and to show that all the gods of the dead in every place of departed spirits throughout Egypt rendered to him homage in one form or another, and in return received benefits from him. And in the second place, the book, being an actual "guide" to the Underworld, with pictures of its various divisions and of the gods and demons of every kind that were to be met with in them, was invaluable for the faithful, who were able to learn from it, whilst they were living upon earth, how to find their way from this world to the next, and how to identify the beings who would attempt to bar their way, and what to say to them. The BOOK ÅM-ṬUAT was a very lengthy work, and a complete copy of it occupied much space whether on walls or on papyrus, and, as poor folk could not afford tombs with chambers and corridors sufficiently large to hold all its texts and pictures, they were obliged to be content with sections, and smaller extracts from it. The need of a shortened form of the work was felt at a comparatively early period after it came into general use, and it is therefore not suprising to find that the priests collected all the facts, which were absolutely essential for the soul that had to travel by itself through the Other World, into a small book that may for convenience be called the "SUMMARY OF ÅM-ṬUAT." In this "Summary" all the lengthy speeches of Åmen-Rā, and the answers of the gods, and, of course, all pictures are omitted.

The oldest copies of the BOOK ÅM-ṬUAT are found in the tombs of Thothmes III., Åmen-ḥetep II., and Åmen-ḥetep III., at Thebes.[1] The most complete and best illustrated copy is that which is found on the walls of

[1] The tombs of Åmen-ḥetep II. and Thothmes III. were discovered by M. Loret in 1898, and, according to the description of them published in the French journals, the copies of Åm-Ṭuat on their walls were in a good state of preservation. The copy of the work in the tomb of Åmen-ḥetep III., written in hieratic, was well preserved in Champollion's time, but is now illegible; see Champollion, *Lettres*, 13e Lettre; and Champollion, *Monuments*, iii. 232-234. The text of the Third Hour was published by Lepsius, *Denkmäler*, iii. 78 and 79. See also *Description de l'Égypte*, Antiq. tom. iii. 193, tom. x., 218, and plates, tom. ii., 80, 81; and Lefébure in *Mémoires Mission Arch. Française*, tom. iii., p. 172.

the tomb of Seti I. at Thebes; here we have eleven out of the twelve sections of the Book Åm-Ṭuat, and the first six divisions of the Summary of the work. The texts and pictures of this fine copy have been completely published by M. Lefébure, assisted by MM. Bouriant, Loret,[1] and Naville, and M. Maspero has translated and discussed the work at length in one of the most important of his luminous dissertations on Egyptian mythology.[2] The next fullest copy is found in the tomb of Rameses VI.,[3] and provides us with eleven divisions, but the drawings are less careful, and the texts are less accurate, and contain numerous additions which appear to represent beliefs of a later period. The history of the Book Åm-Ṭuat shows us that the Egyptians treated it as they treated their older Books of the Dead; they first copied it on the walls of tombs, then on the sides of stone sarcophagi and wooden coffins, and next on rolls of papyrus. We have seen how the kings of the XVIIIth and XIXth Dynasties had it copied on the walls of their tombs, and it must now be noted that Rameses III. decorated his red granite sarcophagus with scenes relating to the course of the sun in the Other World.[4] This sarcophagus is preserved in the Museum

[1] See *Mémoires publiés par les membres de la Miss. Arch. Française*, tom. ii., Paris, 1886.

[2] See *Études de Mythologie et d'Archéologie Egyptiennes*, in *Bibliothèque Égyptologique*, tom. ii., p. 1 ff., Paris, 1893.

[3] See Lefébure, *op. cit.*, tom. iii., fasc. 1, p. 48 ff.

[4] See E. de Rougé, *Notice Sommaire des Monuments Égyptiens exposés dans les Galeries du Musée du Louvre*, Paris, 1876, p. 51.

of the Louvre in Paris, and its cover is in the Fitzwilliam Museum, Cambridge. Among other sarcophagi inscribed with text and pictures from the BOOK ÅM-ṬUAT may be mentioned those of: 1. Horus, son of Taruṭ-en-Sekhet;[1] 2. Tcheṭ-ḥrå, a priest of Ptaḥ;[2] 3. Qem-Ḥāp,[3] the son of Takhāau; and Nekht-neb-f. Now, whilst on the walls of tombs, and on the side of sarcophagi, divisions Nos. I.-XI. are found, the only divisions which are met with on papyrus are Nos. IX.-XII. Thus the Louvre Papyrus, No. 3071, which formed the subject of a special study by Devéria[4] and Pierret,[5] and the Turin Papyrus, published by Lanzone,[6] and the Leyden Papyrus T. 71,[7] contain each the last four divisions only. The Leyden Papyrus T. 72[8] contains divisions X., XI., and XII., the Berlin Papyrus No. 3001 contains divisions IX., X. and XII., and the Berlin Papyrus No. 3005 contains divisions X. and XI. only. There are several papyri in the British Museum inscribed with similar selections.

[1] See E. de Rougé, *Notice Sommaire*, p. 52. It contains the figures of the eleven divisions, with very few inscriptions; see Jéquier, *Le Livre de ce qu'il y a dans l'Hades*, p. 25.

[2] See E. de Rougé, *Notice Sommaire*, p. 52. This sarcophagus is made of basalt, is beautifully cut, and was brought to France by Champollion. See also Sharpe, *Egyptian Inscriptions*, vol. ii., plates 1-24.

[3] See Schäfer in Jéquier, *op. cit.*, p. 26, notes 3 and 4.

[4] See *Catalogue des Manuscrits Égyptiens*, Paris, 1881, p. 15.

[5] See Pierret, *Études Égyptologiques*, tom. ii., p. 103-148.

[6] See Lanzone, *Le Domicile des Esprits*, Paris, 1879, folio.

[7] See *Catalogue du Musée Égyptien de Leyde*, pp. 253-255.

[8] See Jéquier, *op. cit.*, p. 27.

The principal authorities for the text of the SUMMARY of ÅM-ṬUAT are those which M. Jéquier consulted when preparing his edition, viz., the Berlin Papyrus No. 3001, the Leyden Papyrus T. 71, the Louvre Papyrus No. 3071, the Papyrus of Turin, published by Lanzone, and, of course, the tomb of Seti I., which gives the text of the first six divisions. The most valuable of all these is the Leyden Papyrus T. 71, of which an excellent fac-simile, with a complete translation, was published by Drs. Pleyte and Boeser in 1894;[1] in this papyrus the text of the SUMMARY only fills 119 short columns, and the great popularity of the work is attested by the fact that the priests of Åmen were induced to compress all the most important portions of Åm-Ṭuat into so small a compass.

Similar in many details, but widely different from the BOOK ÅM-ṬUAT in point of fundamental doctrine, is the great funeral work to which the names "Book of the Lower Hemisphere,"[2] "Book of Hades," "Livre de l'Enfer," have been given. A glance at the pictures which accompany the texts of this Book is sufficient to show that it deals with the passage of the Sun-god through the Other World during the hours of the night, but, as M. Maspero pointed out long ago, it is wrong to

[1] *Papyrus Funéraire Hiéroglyphique, Shā-ām-Ṭūa* (T. 71). Publié dans la 32ième Livraison des *Monuments Égyptiens du Musée*, Leyden, 1894.

[2] See Devéria, *Catalogue*, Sect. ii., *Le Livre de L'Hémisphère Inférieur.* .

call the region through which the god passes by the name of "Lower Hemisphere," for it suggests that it is below the surface of our earth, which is not the case. There is much to be said also against the titles "Book of Hades," and "Book of Hell," and as among the prominent characteristics which distinguish it from the BOOK ÅM-ṬUAT is a series of gates, it will be convenient and more correct to call it the "BOOK OF GATES." The form in which we first know this work is, clearly, not older than the XVIIIth or XIXth Dynasty, but many parts of it are very much more ancient. As the BOOK ÅM-ṬUAT was composed with the view of asserting the absolute supremacy of Åmen-Rā in the Other World, so the BOOK OF GATES was compiled to prove that, in spite of the pretensions of the priests of Åmen-Rā, Osiris, the ancient god of the dead, was still the over-lord of the Underworld, and that his kingdom was everlasting. The BOOK ÅM-ṬUAT practically ignores Osiris, and is silent even concerning the doctrines of the Judgment and Sekhet-Ḥetepet, and in fact about all the fundamental principles of the religion of Osiris as regards the dead, which had been universally believed throughout Egypt for thousands of years.

The most complete copy of the BOOK OF GATES known to us is found inscribed on the alabaster sarcophagus of Seti I,[1] king of Egypt about B.C. 1375,

[1] See *The Alabaster Sarcophagus of Oimenephtah I., King of Egypt, now in Sir John Soane's Museum, Lincoln's Inn Fields, drawn*

and it consists of two parts:—1. A series of texts and pictures which describe the progress of the Boat of the Sun-god to the kingdom of Osiris, the Judgment of the Dead, the life of the beatified in Sekhet-Ḥetepet, the punishment of the wicked, and the foes of the Sun-god. 2. A series of texts and pictures which represent the magical ceremonies that were performed in very ancient times with the view of reconstructing the body of the Sun, and of making him rise each day. That the BOOK OF GATES embodied many of the most ancient Egyptian religious beliefs and traditions is evident, but it is quite certain that it never became as popular as the BOOK ÅM-ṬUAT; it must always be a matter for wonder that Seti I., having covered several walls in his tomb with the texts of this Book, should fill several more with sections of the BOOK OF GATES, and then have a complete copy of it cut and inlaid on the sides of his alabaster sarcophagus and its cover!

We may now consider the region through which the Sun-god passed during the hours of the night, and the descriptions of its divisions and their inhabitants which are furnished by the BOOK ÅM-ṬUAT

by Joseph Bonomi, and described by Samuel Sharpe, London, 1864. A description of the pictures and texts was given by M. Pierret in the *Revue Archéologique* for 1870; small portions of the text were discussed by Goodwin and Renouf in *Aeg. Zeit.*, 1873, p. 138, and 1874, p. 101; and an English rendering of the whole text was given by E. Lefébure, in the *Records of the Past*, vol. x., p. 79 ff., vol. xii., p. 1 ff.

and the BOOK OF GATES. This region was called by the Egyptians "Ṭat," or "Ṭuat," or "Ṭuaut";[1] the oldest form of the name, and that which is met with in the earliest of the Pyramid Texts is "Ṭat," ; the chief god of the Ṭuat was called "Ṭuat," or "Ṭuaut," , and the beings who lived therein were called "Ṭuatiu," , or . The meaning of the name Ṭat, or Ṭuat, is unknown, and it is useless to speculate upon it or to invent etymologies for it; it was applied to the home of the beatified spirits and the damned, no doubt in predynastic times, and the exact meaning which it conveyed to the minds of those who first used it has been lost. To describe its general situation is less difficult, but not many details as to its exact extent are forthcoming.

To find a word which shall at once describe the situation and character of the Ṭuat is impossible, for the reason that the Egyptian conception of the place of departed spirits is unique. The Ṭuat is not the "Lower Hemisphere," because it is not under the ground, and though for want of a better word I have frequently used "Underworld," when speaking of

[1] The common forms of the names are: , , , , , .

the Ṭuat, it is unsatisfactory, for unless it is specially defined to mean the place of departed spirits in general, it produces a wrong impression in the mind. Again, the word Ṭuat must not be rendered by "Hades," or "Hell," or "Sheol," or "Jehannum," for each of these words has a limited and special meaning. On the other hand, the Ṭuat possessed the characteristics of all these names, for it was an "unseen" place, and it contained abysmal depths of darkness, and there were pits of fire in it wherein the damned, i.e., the enemies of Osiris and Rā, were consumed, and certain parts of it were the homes of monsters in various shapes and forms which lived upon the unfortunate creatures whom they were able to destroy. On the whole, the word Ṭuat may be best rendered by "The Other World,"[1] or "Underworld," always provided that it be clearly understood that the Egyptians never believed it to be under the earth.

In inventing a situation for the Ṭuat the Egyptians appear to have believed that the whole of the habitable world, that is to say, Egypt, was surrounded by a chain of mountains lofty and impassable, just like the Jebel Ḳâf[2] of Muhammadan writers; from one hole in this mountain the sun rose, and in another he set. Outside this chain of mountains, but presumably quite close to them, was the region of the Ṭuat; it ran parallel with

[1] See Maspero, *Études de Mythologie*, tom. ii. p. 27.

[2] See Yâḳûṭ's Geographical Dictionary, ed. Wüstenfeld, tom. iv., page 18.

the mountains, and was on the plane either of the land of Egypt or of the sky above it. On the outside of the Ṭuat was a chain of mountains also, similar to that which encompassed the earth, and so we may say that the Ṭuat had the shape of a valley; and from the fact that it began near the place where the sun set, and ended near the place where he rose, it is permissible to say that the Ṭuat was nearly circular in form. That this is the view taken by the Egyptians themselves is proved by the scene which is reproduced in the BOOK OF GATES (page 303). Here we have the body of Osiris bent round in a circle, and the hieroglyphics enclosed within it declare that it is the Ṭuat. With the identification of Osiris with the Ṭuat we need not deal here, but it is important for our purpose to note that in the time of Seti I. the Egyptians assigned a circular form to the Ṭuat. The view put forward by Signor Lanzone to the effect that the Ṭuat was the place comprised between the arms of the god Shu and the body of the sky-goddess Nut, whom, according to the old legend, he raised up from the embrace of her husband the Earth-god Seb, so forming the earth and the sky, thus appears to be untenable.[1]

Now as the Ṭuat was situated on the other side of the mountains which separated it from Egypt, and from the sun, moon, and stars which lighted the skies of that country, it follows that it must have been a region which was shrouded in the gloom and darkness of night,

[1] See Lanzone, *Le domicile des Esprits*, p. 1.

and a place of fear and horror. At each end of the Ṭuat was a space which was neither wholly darkness nor wholly light, the western end being partially lighted by the setting sun, and the eastern end by the rising sun. From the pictures in the BOOK ÁM-ṬUAT and the BOOK OF GATES we learn that a river flowed through the Ṭuat, much as the Nile flowed through Egypt, and we see that there were inhabitants on each of its banks, just as there were human beings on each side of the Nile. At one place the river of the Ṭuat joined the great celestial waters which were supposed to form the source of the earthly Nile.

How, or when, or where the belief arose it is impossible to say, but it seems that at a very early period the inhabitants of Egypt thought that the souls of the dead when they departed from this world made their way into the Ṭuat, and took up their abode there, and long before the Dynastic Period the Ṭuat was regarded throughout Egypt as the kingdom of the dead. Certain sections of it were considered to belong by traditional right to certain cities, e.g., Heliopolis, Memphis, Herakleopolis, Abydos, etc., each possessing its own "Other World" and gods of the dead, and all these had to be considered by the theologians who formulated general plans of the Ṭuat. How the Egyptians imagined the dead to live in the Ṭuat, or upon what, is not clear, but they seem to have thought that all their wants could be provided for by the use of words of power, amulets, talismans, etc. In the earliest times of all the souls of the dead remained in the "Other World" which belonged to their town or city, but when Osiris attained to the supreme power over the dead, it was only natural that departed spirits should flock from all parts of Egypt to his kingdom, wherein the beatified enjoyed a life very much like that which they had lived upon earth. The celestial kingdom of Osiris, that is to say, Sekhet-Ḥetepet or Sekhet-Ȧaru, was originally a copy of some very fertile region in the Delta, and, to the very end of the period of native Egyptian rule, the Egyptian Paradise consisted of green fields intersected by streams of living, i.e., running water, with abundant crops of wheat and barley, and its appearance represented a typical middle-Delta landscape. So long as Osiris had his kingdom in the Delta, probably near the ancient city of Mendes, the souls of the dead travelled from south to north, but at a later period, when Osiris had absorbed the position and attributes of KHENT-ȦMENTI, perhaps the oldest god of the dead of Abydos, departed spirits made their way from north to south, so that they might enter the Ṭuat by the "Gap" in the mountains there. Still later, the Egyptians reverted to their old belief as to the situation of the domain of Osiris, and the books which deal with the Ṭuat always assume that it lies far away to the north, and were intended to guide souls on their way to it.

The ultimate fate of the souls of human beings who had departed to the Ṭuat must always have been a matter of speculation to the Egyptians, and at the best they could only *hope* that they had traversed the long, dark, and dangerous valley in safety. The same may be said of numbers of the gods, who in very early times were believed to possess a nature which closely resembled that of men and women, and to be in danger of extermination in the Ṭuat. Of the gods the only one about whose successful passage of the Ṭuat there was no doubt was Rā, or according to the priests of Ȧmen, Ȧmen-Rā, for he rose each morning in the East, and it was manifest to all that he had overcome whatsoever dangers had threatened him in the Ṭuat during the past night. This being so, it became the object of every man to obtain permission to travel in the boat of Rā through the Ṭuat, for those who were followers of Osiris could disembark when it arrived at his kingdom, and those who wished to remain with Rā for ever could remain in it with him. To each class of believer a guide to the Ṭuat was necessary, for up to a certain place in that region both the followers of Osiris and the followers of Rā required information about the divisions of the Ṭuat, and knowledge of the names of the Halls and Gates, and of the beings who guarded them and who were all-powerful in the land of darkness. For the worshippers of Ȧmen, or Ȧmen-Rā, the BOOK ȦM-ṬUAT was prepared, whilst the followers of Osiris pinned their faith to the BOOK OF GATES. From each of these Books we find that the Sun-god was not able to pass through the Ṭuat by virtue of the powers which he possessed as the great god of the world, but only through his knowledge of the proper words of power, and of magical names and formulae, before the utterance of which every denizen of the Ṭuat was powerless. Osiris had, of course, passed through the Ṭuat, and seated himself on his throne in the "House of Osiris," but even he would have been unable to perform his journey in safety through the Ṭuat without the help of the words of power which "Horus, the son of Isis, the son of Osiris," had uttered, and the magical ceremonies which he had performed. Words and ceremonies alike he learned from Isis, who, according to a later tradition, obtained the knowledge of them from Thoth, the Divine Intelligence. Now if Osiris and Rā had need of such magical assistance in their passage through the Ṭuat, how much greater must have been the need of man!

The Ṭuat was, according to the authors of the funeral works of the XVIIIth and XIXth Dynasties, divided into twelve portions, some of which are called "SEKHET" , i.e., "Field," others "NUT" , i.e., "City," others "ĀRRIT" , i.e., "Hall," and others "QERRET" 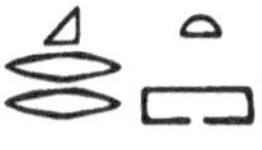, i.e., "Circle." The first indicates that the region to which it was applied was believed to consist of cultivated lands, the second suggests a place where there were many buildings and houses, the third a territory which was vast and spacious, and which, in some respects, represented an empty courtyard, or hall, or compound of a house, and the fourth probably describes the circular form of some divisions. Now since the Ṭuat was traversed by the sun-god during the hours of the night, the Egyptians regarded each of these divisions as the equivalent of an hour, and hence it came that the sections of the Books of the Ṭuat were often called "Hours," the First Hour corresponding to the First Division, and so on up to the Twelfth Hour. It will, however, be urged that during the summer in Egypt the night is not twelve hours long, but the answer to this objection is that the first division is in reality only the ante-chamber of the Ṭuat, and the twelfth the ante-chamber of the sky of this world, into which the Sun-god enters to begin the new day. The divisions II. to XI. of the Ṭuat have an entirely different character from the ante-chamber of the Ṭuat and that of the sky.

It has already been said that a river flows from one end of the Ṭuat to the other, and its existence can only be explained in one way. At a very early period of their history the Egyptians believed that the Sun-god passed over the sky, which they held to be a vast watery mass, in some kind of boat; the belief in the existence of such a boat was absolutely necessary, for unless the fire of the sun was protected from contact with the water of the sky, it would, they argued, be extinguished. So far back as the period when the Pyramids of Gîza were built, the existence of two boats was assumed; in one, called MĀṬET, the Sun-god sailed from the time he rose until noon, and in the other, called SEKTET, he sailed from noon to sunset. When the conception of the existence of the Ṭuat was evolved, and the belief that the Sun-god passed through it each night gained credence, it became necessary to find some means of transport for the god. It was impossible to remove him from his boat, which was, like himself, eternal, hence its name, "Boat of Millions of Years," and even if it had been possible the difficulty remained either of taking his boat back from the place of sunset to the place of sunrise, so that it might be ready for him on the following morning when he emerged from the Ṭuat, or of providing him with a new boat each day. The simplest way was to assume in the Ṭuat the existence of a river which was in direct communication with the watery mass of the sky on which Rā sailed by day, and to make the Sun-god to enter the Ṭuat on it. This was the natural way out of the difficulty, for apart from the fact that no other means of transport for the god could be devised, it was consistent with experience that kings, and nobles, and high officials, always travelled through Egypt by water. No animal and no chariot could convey the god through the Ṭuat, for, even had animals or chariots suitable for the purpose existed, they must have been consumed by the god's fire. We shall see later that there was one division of the Ṭuat through which the Sun-god could not pass even in his boat, and that he was obliged to leave it and travel on the back of a serpent.

From the titles of the Book Ȧm Ṭuat, as it is found in the tomb of Seti I., we may gather that the pictures accompanying the texts were supposed to be exact copies of the divisions of the Ṭuat as they actually existed in Amenti, i.e., the "hidden place," or the "Other World," and the texts were supposed to give the traveller in the Ṭuat all the information he could possibly require concerning the "souls, the gods, the shadows, the spirits, the gods of the Ṭuat, the gates of the Ṭuat, the hours and their gods, and the gods who praise Rā, and those who carry out his edicts of destruction." The divisions of the Ṭuat according to this work are:—

Division I. *Names*—Maāti, 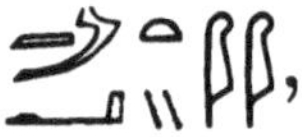, and Net-Rā, 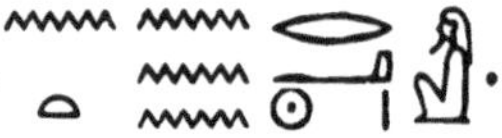.

Warder—Ȧrnebȧui, .

Hour-goddess—Ushem-ḥātiu-kheftiu-nu-Rā, .

Division II. *Name*—Urnes, 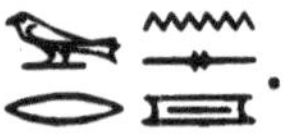.

Warder—Ȧm-nebȧui, 

.

Hour-goddess—Seshet-māket-neb-s,

.

Division III. *Name*—NET-NEB-UĀ-KHEPER-ĀUT,

Warder—KHETRȦ, 

Hour-goddess—ṬENT-BAIU, 

Division IV. *Name* — ĀNKHET-KHEPERU, 

Name of the gate of this Circle—ȦMENT-SETHAU, 

Hour-goddess—URT-EM-SEKHEMU-S,

Division V. *Name*—ȦMENT, 

Name of the gate of this Circle—ĀḤĀ-NETERU, 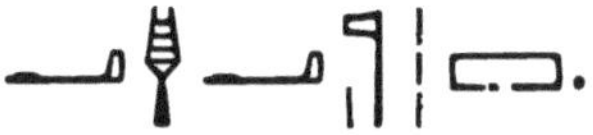

Hour-goddess—SEKMET-ḤER-ȦBT-UȦA-S,

Division VI. *Name*—METCHET-NEBT-ṬUAT,

Name of the gate of this City—SEPṬ-METU, 

Hour-goddess—MESPERIT - ÀR - ĀT - MAĀTU, 

Division VII. *Name*—TEPḤET-SHETAT, 

Name of the gate of this City—RUTI-EN-ÀSÀR, 

Hour-goddess--KHESFET-HÀU-ḤESQETU-NEḤA - ḤRÀ, 

Division VIII. *Name*—ṬEBAT-NETERU-S, 

Name of the Gate—ĀḤĀ-ÀN-URṬ-NEF, 

Hour - goddess — NEBT - USHA, 

Division IX. *Name*—BEST - ÀRU - ĀNKHET - KHEPERU, 

Name of the Gate—SA - EM - ḲEB, [1]

[1] Or, SA-AḲEB, reading  for .

Hour-goddess—ṬUATET-MĀKTET-EN-NEB-S, 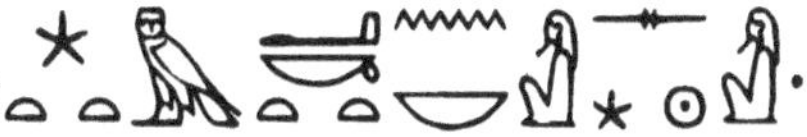

Division X. *Name*—METET-QA-UTCHEBU, 

Name of the Gate—ĀA-KHEPERU-MES-ÅRU, 

Hour-goddess—ṬENṬENIT-UḤETES-KHAK-ÅB, 

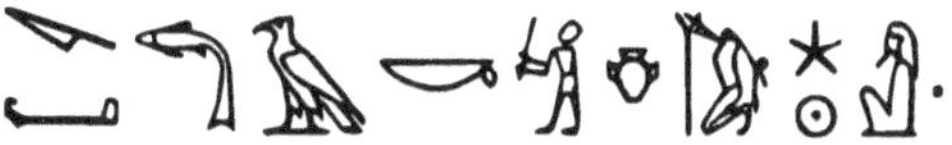

Division XI. *Name*—RE-EN-QERERT-ÅPT-KHATU, 

Name of the Gate—SEKHEN-ṬUATIU, 

Hour-goddess—SEBIT-NEBT-UÅA-KHESFET-SEBÅ-EM-PERT-F, 

Division XII. *Name*—KHEPER-KEKIU-KHĀU-MEST, 

Name of the Gate—THEN-NETERU,

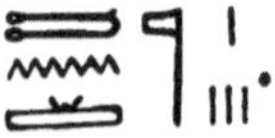

Hour-goddess — MAA-NEFERT-RĀ,

The divisions of the Ṭuat according to the BOOK OF GATES are usually marked by Gates, which are guarded by serpents; they are as follows:—

Division I. *Name of Guardian Gods.*—SET and TAT.

Name of the Region.—SET-ÅMENTET,

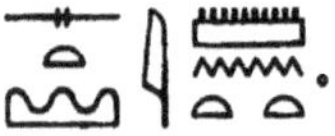 Western Vestibule.

Division II. *Name of the Serpent* — SAA-SET,

Division III. *Name of the Serpent* — AQEBI,

Name of the Gate—SEPṬET-UAUAU,

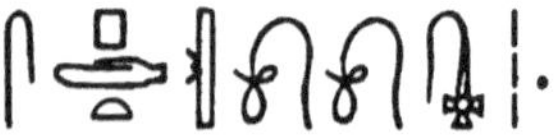

Division IV. *Name of the Serpent* — TCHEṬBI,

Name of the Gate—NEBT-S-TCHEFAU,

Division V. *Name of the Serpent*—TEKA-ḤRÂ, .

Name of the Gate—ÂRIT, .

Division VI. At the entrance to this division is the Judgment Hall of Osiris.

Name of the Serpent—SET-EM-MAAT-F,

.

Name of the Gate — NEBT - ĀḤĀ,

.

Division VII. *Name of the Serpent*—AKHA-EN-MAAT,

.

Name of the Gate—PESṬIT, .

Division VIII. *Name of the Serpent* — SET - ḤRÂ,

.

Name of the Gate — BEKHKHI,

.

Division IX. *Name of the Serpent*—ĀB-TA, .

Name of the Gate—ĀAT-SHEFSHEFT,

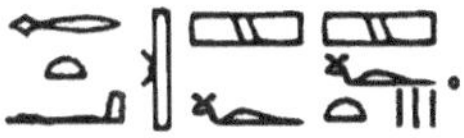.

Division X. *Name of the Serpent*—SETHU, .

Name of the Gate — TCHESERIT,

.

Division XI. *Name of the Serpent*—ÅM-NETU-F,

Name of the Gate—SHETAT-BESU,

Division XII. *Names of the Serpents*—SEBI, ,

and RERI, .

Name of the Gate — ṬESERT-BAIU,

 Eastern Vestibule.

From the above lists it is clear that in the BOOK ÅM-ṬUAT the actual divisions of the Ṭuat are considered without any reference to Gates, even if such existed in the scheme of the priests of Åmen-Rā, and that according to the Book of Gates, the Gates of the divisions in the Ṭuat are the most important and most characteristic features. The absence of Gates in the BOOK ÅM-ṬUAT is not difficult to explain; the compilers of this work, wishing to exalt Åmen-Rā, did away with the Gates, which were the most important features of the kingdom of Osiris, so that the necessity for Åmen-Rā to seek permission of their warders, who were appointed by Osiris, was obviated.

CHAPTER V.

THE CONTENTS OF THE BOOK ÅM-ṬUAT AND THE BOOK OF GATES COMPARED.

THE WESTERN VESTIBULE OR ANTECHAMBER OF THE ṬUAT.

HAVING already briefly described the general character of the BOOK ÅM-ṬUAT and the BOOK OF GATES we may pass at once to the comparison of their contents. For the sake of convenience, in describing the various divisions of the Ṭuat let us assume that we are occupying the position of a disembodied spirit who is about to undertake the journey through the Ṭuat, and that we are standing at the entrance to the First Division awaiting the arrival of the BOAT OF THE SUN-GOD, on which we hope to have permission to travel. Every funeral rite has been duly and adequately performed, the relatives and friends of the deceased have made the legally appointed offerings, and said all the prayers proper for the occasion, amulets inscribed with magical names and formulae have been attached to the body, copies of sacred writings have been laid on it or near it in the tomb, the priests have said the final words which will secure for the soul a passage in the Boat of Rā, and a safe-conduct to the abode of the blessed, whether this abode be in the boat itself or in the kingdom of Osiris. The result of all these things is that we have been enabled to pass through the tomb out into the region which lies immediately to the west of the mountain-chain on the west bank of the Nile, which we may consider as one mountain and call Manu,[1] or the mountain of the Sunset. At this place are gathered together numbers of spirits, all bent on making their way to the abode of the blessed; these are they who have departed from their bodies during the day, and they have made their way to the sacred place in Western Thebes where they can join the Boat of the Sun-god.

Some are adequately equipped with words of power, and amulets, and their ultimate safety is assured, but others are less well provided, and it will be the fate of many of these to remain in the place wherein they now are, and never to enter the House of Osiris or the Boat of Rā. They will not suffer in any way whatsoever, but will simply remain there, protecting themselves as best they can by any words of power they may possess until such time as they are overcome by some hostile being, when they will die and take their places among the other dead spirits, having failed to present themselves in the Judgment Hall of Osiris.

[1] In Egyptian, , or, .

Now the dead who are in the various divisions of the Ṭuat do not, apparently, pass entirely out of existence; for, as we shall see later, they are revivified once each day by light which the Sun-god casts upon them as he passes through the Ṭuat, and for a season they enjoy his rays, and when, as he leaves one division to enter another, the Gate closes upon him, and shuts out his light, they set up dismal cries at his departure, and then sink down into inertness in the darkness which will swallow them up for twenty-four hours. It is possible that the dead here referred to represent the primitive inhabitants of the country, and the gods of the dead whom they worshipped when on earth, but there is no doubt that to these were joined the spirits of those who for some reason or other failed to advance beyond one or other of the divisions of the Ṭuat.

Now, however, the time of evening has come, and the Sun-god in the SEKTET BOAT, wherein he has travelled since noon, draws nigh, flooding the FIRST DIVISION of the Ṭuat with light. This DIVISION, or ante-chamber, or vestibule, of the Ṭuat is, according to the BOOK ÂM-ṬUAT, called NET-RĀ, and before the Sun-god can come to the dweller in the Ṭuat he must pass over a space which is said to be 120, or 220, *àtru*, or leagues, in length. The river URNES, on which the boat moves, is 300 *atru* in extent, and is divided into two portions. On looking into the BOAT OF THE SUN-GOD we see that this deity has transformed himself, and that he no longer appears as a fiery disk, but as a ram-headed man, who stands within a shrine; in other words, Rā has taken the form of Osiris, in order that he may pass successfully through the kingdom of the dead, whose lord and god is Osiris. The name given to this form is ȦF, or ȦFU, , which means literally "flesh," and "a dead body;" it was as a dead body that Osiris first entered the Ṭuat, and those who wished to become what he became subsequently had to enter the Ṭuat as dead bodies and with the attributes wherewith he entered it. The boat then contains the body of the dead Sun-god, or ȦFU-RĀ; he has with him a crew of seven gods and one goddess; one of these acts as guide (ȦP-UAT), another as steersman, another as the "look out," and the goddess, or "lady of the boat," is there as representative of the Division through which they are about to pass. Besides these we have KA-SHU, i.e., the "double of Shu," the god of the atmosphere of this world, who is present in the boat in order to supply the god with air; ḤERU-ḤEKENU, who recites magical formulae; and SA and ḤU, who represent the knowledge and intelligence necessary for the due performance of the journey. We may note that the boat moves by itself, and that the gods who form a procession in front of it do not tow it. As we have already described these in vol. i. (see pp. 4-8), it is needless to say here more than that they are all forms of the Sun-god, or deified aspects of him, and that they accompany their lord, who has transformed himself. Side by side with the boat of

ÅFU-RĀ is a smaller boat, in which the coming into being of Osiris is depicted, and the beetle is there to typify the presence of Osiris, and to lead ÅFU-RĀ on his way through the DIVISION (vol. i., p. 7). As ÅFU-RĀ is preceded by a number of forms of the Sun-god, so the "form of Osiris," KHEPER-EN-ÅSÅR, is preceded by a number of Osirian deities, three snakes and three goddesses, among them being NEITH of the NORTH, NEITH of the SOUTH, and the rare goddess ÅRTET (vol. i., p. 7).

The direction in which ÅFU-RĀ is moving is northwards, and we may glance at the beings who are on the banks of the river of the Ṭuat. On the right hand are nine apes, "which sing to Rā as he entereth the Ṭuat," nine gods and twelve goddesses, who sing praises unto Rā, and twelve serpents, which belch forth the fire that gives light to lighten the god on his way (vol. i., pp. 12-15). On the left hand are nine apes, "which open the gates to the Great Soul" (i.e. ÅFU-RĀ), twelve goddesses, who open the gates in the earth, twelve goddesses, who guide the god, and nine gods, "who praise Rā" (vol. i., pp. 9-11). So soon as ÅFU-RĀ has entered this DIVISION (ĀRRIT) he calls upon the gods to let him proceed, and he asks for light and guidance from them; he bids one set of apes to open the doors to him, and the other to welcome him. As he is provided not only with the word of power, but has also the knowledge how to utter it, the gods straightway bid him enter the place where OSIRIS

KHENTI-ÅMENTI dwells. The serpent goddesses sing hymns to him, and they lighten the darkness by pouring out fire from their mouths, the god takes possession of the grain which is in NET-RĀ, his word has its due effect upon every one, and the punishments which he adjudges to the condemned are carried out duly. As for the dead who are in this DIVISION they do not journey on with the god, but they are left behind (vol. i., p. 8), and when they see him pass through the fortified gate which guards the entrance to the SECOND DIVISION "they wail" (vol i., p. 20). The texts say nothing about the actual condition of the dead whom ÅFU-RĀ leaves behind him, and nothing of the place, or places, whence they came; we can only assume that they are those who for some reason or other have failed to obtain a seat in the BOAT of the god. They must not be confounded with the gods and goddesses and apes who are in attendance upon ÅFU-RĀ, for these are, in reality, officers of the Division whose duty it is to escort him to the Gate of the Second Division, and then to return to their places to await his return the following evening. In return for their services they receive food and drink by the command of the god. As the Boat of ÅFU-RĀ was assumed by the priests of Amen-Rā to begin its journey through the Ṭuat at Thebes, and as we are expressly told that the god was obliged to pass over a space of 120 or 220 *åtru*, or leagues, before he came to the dwellers in the Ṭuat, it is probable that the first group of dead are those who entered the Ṭuat through the opening in the mountains behind Abydos, which was called the "GAP." The oldest god of the dead of Abydos was KHENTI-ȦMENTI, i.e., Governor of Ȧmenti, ȦMENTI, i.e., the "hidden" land, being a name for the Underworld, or "Other World," in general. This being so, it is clear that when ȦFU-RĀ came to the end of the FIRST DIVISION of the Ṭuat he arrived at the beginning of the dominions of KHENTI-ȦMENTI, whose attributes became absorbed subsequently into those of OSIRIS.

In the BOOK OF GATES the FIRST DIVISION is depicted in a different manner. The BOAT OF THE SUN is seen passing through the mountain of the horizon, which is divided into two parts; the god appears in the form of a beetle within a disk, which is surrounded by a serpent with voluminous folds. The only gods with him in the boat are SA and ḤEKA, here the personifications of the intelligence and the word of power. The duty of SA is to make all plans for the god's journey, and ḤEKA will utter the words of power which will enable him to overcome all opposition. On each half of the mountain is a sceptre, one having the head of a jackal, and the other that of a ram; each sceptre is supported by the god TAT and the god SET, the personifications of the Ṭuat and the Mountain respectively. One sceptre is mentioned in the text, which is somewhat obscure in meaning; it seems, however, that the jackal-headed sceptre uttered words on behalf of the god ȦFU-RĀ, and that the other typified him, taking the place of the ram-headed god with a human body which we have in the BOOK ÀM-ṬUAT. On each side of the Boat are twelve gods, who presumably represent the Twelve Hours of the Day, and the Twelve Hours of the Night; one group is called "Neteru Set" (*or* Semt), i.e., "Gods of the Mountain," and the other "Neteru Set-Àmentet," i.e., "Gods of the Mountain of the Hidden Land." The gods of the Mountain are the offspring of Rā himself, and they "emerged from his eye" (vol. ii., p. 85), and to them has Àmentet been given as an abode.

CHAPTER VI.

SECOND DIVISION OF THE ṬUAT.

I. The Kingdom of Khenti-Ȧmenti-Osiris according to the Book Ȧm-Ṭuat.

The god Ȧfu-Rā now enters the region Urnes , which derives its name from that of the river flowing through it; it is 309, or 480 *ȧtru* or leagues in length, and 120 wide. Urnes is a portion of the dominions of Osiris-Khenti-Ȧmenti, the great god of Abydos, and it, no doubt, formed a section of the Sekhet-ḥetepet according to the old theology of Egypt. The Boat of Ȧfu-Rā is now under the direction of the goddess of the second hour of the night, Shesat-māket-neb-s, and the uraei of Isis and Nephthys have been added to its crew. Immediately in front of it are four boats, which move by themselves; the first contains the full moon, of which Osiris was a form, the second the emblem of a deity of harvest, the third the symbols of another agricultural deity, and the fourth the Grain-god personified. All four boats contain either forms or symbols of Osiris, in his different aspects, as the god of ploughing, sowing, and reaping, and of the grain from the time when it germinates to the season of harvest.

When Ȧfu-Rā has come into Urnes, he addresses the gods of the region, who are called "Baiu-Ṭuatiu," and tells them to open their doors so that they may receive air, and fresh food, and fresh water, in return for the deeds of valour which they have done on behalf of Ȧfu-Rā. It seems that at one portion of this Division the followers of Osiris and Rā had to do battle against Āpep and his friends, and that in return for their services the god gave them places here in which to dwell, with an abundance of wheat and barley, etc. The gods in reply welcome Ȧfu-Rā, and beg him to dissipate the darkness in Ȧmenti, and to slay the serpents Ḥau and Neḥa-ḥrȧ (vol. i., p. 40); they promise that those who guide his boat shall destroy Āpep, that Osiris shall come to meet him and shall avenge him, and that he shall rest in Ȧment, and shall appear in the East the following morning under the form of Kheperȧ. After this speech they lead Ȧfu-Rā into a state of peace in Sekhet-en-pertiu, , i.e., the "Field of the Gods of grain," wherein are the boats of the Grain-gods already described. In this fair haven Ȧfu-Rā rests, and every follower of Osiris hoped to follow his example.

If we consider for a moment the group of divine beings which stands on each bank of the river Urnes it becomes evident that each god or goddess belongs to the company of Osiris. To the right of the boat stand six gods, who either hold or wear an ear of corn and are connected with the growth of the grain (vol. i., p. 31), gods armed with knives, and connected with the harvest, gods of the seasons, each holding a notched palm-stick, the god of the year, the gods of SOTHIS and ORION (vol. i., p. 32) Osiris-Unnefer, Akhabit, Anubis, the "Eater of the Ass,"[1] etc. To the left of the Boat are six deities, each with a phallus in the form of a knife, the double god HORUS-SET (vol. i., p. 29), various animal- and bird-headed gods, goddesses both with and without uraei on their heads, the "Crook" (*mest* ) of Osiris, the serpent-protector of Osiris, and so on. The gods on the right of ÅFU-RĀ are they who give him "the seasons, and the years which are in their hands," and so soon as he speaks to them "they have life through his voice"; he, moreover, tells them what to do, and he orders that the herbs of the field of URNES shall be given to them in abundance.

Nekht spearing the Eater of the Ass.

The duties of these gods are simple: they supply

[1] This is a name given to the serpent which is seen attacking an ass in the XIth Chapter of the Book of the Dead, and which is a form of the god Set; the Ass is probably a form of the sun-god Rā. THE EATER OF THE GREAT PHALLUS, i.e., the Ass, was also a power of evil, yet here he is found seated among beneficent gods.

the followers of ÅFU-RĀ, i.e., those spirits who have succeeded in entering his boat, with green herbs, they give them water, and they light the fires which are to destroy the enemies of Rā. It is not, however, easy to understand their position. All these gods are under the rule of ÅM-NEBÅUI, who is "the lord of this Field," but it seems that they remain in a state of inertness until ÅFU-RĀ enters and shines upon them; and although they have their duties and know how to perform them, it is suggested by the texts that they perform nothing until he speaks to them. In other words, they are merely dead gods, until the word of power spoken by ÅFU-RĀ makes them produce grain on which to feed themselves and the "followers of Rā." In this way is the power of Åmen-Rā shown: his dead body, i.e., the night sun, is able to re-vivify all the gods of the kingdom of Osiris, and to make them work. The gods on the left have, first of all, to praise ÅFU-RĀ after he has entered URNES; they next "guard the day, and bring on the night until the great god cometh out into the East of the sky." Besides this their duty is to bring to the god's notice the words of those who are upon earth, and they make souls to come to their forms (vol. i., p. 34); they are also concerned with the "offerings of the night," and effect the overthrow of enemies.

From this passage it is clear that the Egyptians believed that words uttered on earth were taken to ÅFU-RĀ by his ministers, and it is difficult not to think that such words must have been in the form of petitions, or prayers, if only for sepulchral offerings. So soon as ÅFU-RĀ has passed through the Division, and his light has begun to leave them, all the gods of URNES "cry out in lamentation, and utter wailings because he has left them." From the SUMMARY of the BOOK ÅM-ṬUAT we gather that the pictures and texts referring to this Division of the Ṭuat, or Hour of the night, were believed to possess special efficacy, and the faithful thought that if a man knew the names of its gods he would receive a place of abode in URNES, and would travel about with the god, would have the power of entering the earth and the Ṭuat and of going so far as the pillars which supported the heavens, would travel over the serpent ĀMU-ĀA (i.e., the Eater of the Ass), would eat the bread intended for the Boat of the Earth,[1] and would partake of the perfumed unguent of the god TATUBÅ. Moreover, it is stated that the man who makes offerings to the BAIU-ṬUATIU (i.e., the divine souls of the Ṭuat), mentioning them by their names, shall in very truth receive innumerable benefits upon earth. The texts giving these facts are most important, for they prove that in early times the abode of the blessed was believed to be in URNES, and that the making of offerings to the dead was inculcated as a meritorious act, and that it was believed to bring blessings upon him that made the offering even whilst he was upon earth. It may also be noted in passing

[1] See within, page 126.

that the heaven URNES was somewhat exclusive, for only the followers of Osiris and Rā were admitted.

SECOND DIVISION OF THE ṬUAT.

II. THE KINGDOM OF KHENTI-ÀMENTI-OSIRIS ACCORDING TO THE BOOK OF GATES.

To advance into this Division the Boat of ÀFU-RĀ must first pass through the Gate which is guarded by the huge serpent SAA-SET, and this done the god now takes upon himself the form in which he appears in the BOOK ÀM-ṬUAT, i.e., that of a ram-headed man. The snake-goddess MEḤEN, which surrounded the disk enclosing a beetle, now envelops the shrine in which he stands; it must be noted that SA and ḤEKAU stand, as before, in the Boat, which is now towed along by four gods of the Ṭuat, who represent the four quarters of the earth and the four cardinal points. The Boat is received by a company of thirteen gods, who are apparently under the rule of a god who holds a staff. The object of the visit of ÀFU-RĀ is to "weigh words "and deeds in Àment, to make a distinction between "the great and little gods, to assign thrones to the "Spirits [who are pure], to dismiss the damned to the "place set apart for them, and to destroy their bodies." (vol. ii., p. 91). Now this is an important statement, for it distinctly implies that a judgment of the dead takes place in the Second Division, or Hour, of the Ṭuat, which is here called ȦMENT, that the positions of the dead are graded, and that reward and punishment are meted out to the dead, according to their deserts. It is said by ȦFU-RĀ to the dwellers in ȦMENT, "the dead "(*mitu* ) shall not enter in after you"; which proves that, wherever the place of punishment was, it was not in the SECOND Division of the Ṭuat. The gods who assist ȦFU-RĀ in his work of judgment are said to live upon the offerings made to them upon earth; here was a direct inducement to the faithful to make offerings regularly to the gods of the Ṭuat, and it was understood that such acts of piety would tell on their behalf when their words and deeds came to be weighed in Ȧment. The reader will note that it is ȦFU-RĀ who is the judge here, and not Osiris.

Examining now the beings who are on both banks of the river we see that they fall naturally into two classes, viz., the good and the bad; the former are on the right hand of the god, and the latter on his left, just as saints and sinners are arraigned before God's throne in mediaeval pictures of the Judgment. The good are divided into two classes, "the ḤETEPTIU who "praise Rā," and the "MAĀTIU who dwell in the Ṭuat" (vol. ii., p. 93). The ḤETEPTIU are thus called because they made "offerings" (*ḥetepet*) to Rā upon earth, and burned incense to him; they also sang praises to Rā and worshipped him upon earth, and uttered *ḥekau*, or words of power, against ĀPEP, the arch-foe of Rā (vol. ii., p. 94). From this text we see that it was not enough for the followers of Rā to praise him and give him gifts, but that they must also use magical words and formulae in order that Rā's foe may be destroyed; and, because when they were upon earth they made offerings to the Ṭuat-gods, now that they are themselves in the Ṭuat and have need of food, Rā declares that offerings made to them shall never fail, and their souls shall never be destroyed. The MAĀTIU beings have this name given to them because, as the text says, "they spoke *Maāt*," i.e., what is true, "upon earth"; moreover, "they did not approach the *neterit*," 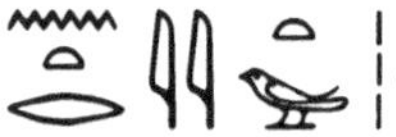. Now the word *neterit* usually means "goddesses," but here it has an unusual determinative, which, however, suggests that it is used to express some idea of "evil" in connexion with the gods or goddesses, such as blasphemy, or contempt, or apostacy. On the whole it seems most likely that *neterit* means "false gods," that is to say, gods whom Rā would not recognize as such, and that the feminine form of the word, with the unusual determinative, indicates they were weak and miserable beings. As a reward for their veracity and orthodoxy (?) upon earth, the food on which they live is *Maāt*, i.e., truth, and they themselves become *Maāt*, or TRUTH itself, and they are permitted to invoke the god in the Gate. Rā, moreover, gives them the mastery over the waters of the region, which, though cool and refreshing to the MAĀTIU beings themselves, become "waters of fire" (vol. ii., p. 95) to those who are sinners and are involved in wickedness. We have already seen that the wicked were not allowed to enter this Division, therefore it appears that it was held to be possible for the dead round about it to attempt to drink of the cool waters, which straightway turned into fire and consumed them.

Turning now to those beings who stand to the left of the Boat (vol. ii., pp. 96-99), we see that they are twenty-four in number; of these four lie dead, or helpless, and are called ENENIU, i.e., the "Inert," and twenty stand with their backs bowed, and their arms tied at their elbows behind them, in an agonizing position. Here, it is clear, are beings who are fettered and stand awaiting their doom. The charges made against them are to the effect that: 1. They blasphemed Rā upon earth. 2. They invoked evil upon him that was in the Egg. 3. They thrust aside the right. 4. They spoke against KHUTI. The god referred to as being "in the Egg" is, of course, a form of the Sun-god, and we know from the LIVth Chapter of the Book of the Dead, that the EGG was laid by ḲENḲENUR, or the "Great Cackler." The god KHUTI is the form of the Sun-god at sunrise and sunset, and thus we see that all the sins which were committed by the ENENIU and their fettered companions were against Rā, and against forms of him. The name given to these is "STAU," i.e., "Apostates of the Hall of Rā," and sentence of doom is passed upon them by TEMU on behalf of Rā; it is decreed that their arms shall never be untied again, that their bodies shall be cut to pieces, and that their souls shall cease to exist (vol. ii., p. 97). Such are the things which take place in the Second Division of the Ṭuat according to the BOOK OF GATES, and, view them in whatever way we may, it is impossible not to conclude that the Egyptians thought that those who praised and worshipped Rā upon earth were rewarded with good things, whilst those who treated him lightly were punished. It is evident also that the offering up of propitiatory sacrifices and making of peace offerings were encouraged by the religion of Osiris, as being good both for gods and men.

CHAPTER VII.

THIRD DIVISION OF THE ṬUAT.

I. The Kingdom of Khenti-Ȧmenti-Osiris, according to the Book Ȧm-Ṭuat.

The Boat of Ȧfu-Rā, leaving the abode of the Souls of the Ṭuat, now enters that of the Baiu-shetaiu, or the "Secret Souls," and we find that a change has taken place as regards the crew. The goddess of the hour called Ṭent-baiu has taken charge of the Boat, a hawk-headed god acts as steersman, and the number of the other gods is reduced to four. The region now entered by Ȧfu-Rā is called Net-neb-uā-kheper-āut, and it is 309 (or 480) *ȧtru* or leagues in length, and 120 in width; it is, in fact, a continuation of the domains of Osiris, and in it is the House of Ṭeṭ wherein the great god of the dead himself dwells. The Boat of Ȧfu-Ra is preceded by three boats (vol. i., pp. 45-47) of a mystical character, containing hawk-gods, and mummied forms of gods who are akin to Osiris. Facing the boats are four forms of Osiris, with their arms and hands covered. Having arrived in this Division, Ȧfu-Rā cries out to its god, Osiris, who straightway creates these secret boats and sends them to bring ȦFU-RĀ to the place where he is. The abode of Osiris is situated on the NET-ȦSȦR, , i.e., the "Stream of Osiris," a name given to the river of the Ṭuat in the THIRD DIVISION, and it is at the head of this river that the throne of Osiris rests according to some copies of the Theban Recension of the Book of the Dead. The inhabitants who are seen on both banks of the stream are called PERTIU, , and they live on lands which have been allotted to them by Ȧfu-Rā; in return for these they serve Osiris and defend him from the attacks of all his enemies. As the boat in which ȦFU-Rā stands and the three other boats move on, the gods on the banks move with them and guard them, and when they have escorted the great god to the end of their territory, they return to their old places and await his coming on the following night.

On the right of ȦFU-RĀ are twenty-six gods, and of these eight are forms of Osiris, four of Osiris of the North, and four of Osiris of the South; all are under the rule of KHETRȦ, who is the "Warder of this Field" (vol. i., p. 60), but it is only when they hear the words of AFU-RĀ that they come to life. The work which they do in this region is to hew and hack souls in pieces, to imprison the shadows of the dead, and to carry out the sentence of death on those who are doomed to destruction in a place of fire; they cause fires to come into being, and flames to burst forth on the wicked.

Now in this case also the beings who are doomed to be burned in a place specially set apart for this purpose cannot be of the number of the gods who protect Osiris, for they were created by Rā to serve this god in this Division of the Ṭuat, and to attend upon himself as he made his journey through it each day! They must, then, be the dead of olden time who have reached this Division, but who through want of friends and relatives upon earth to make proper and sufficient offerings daily, or through some other cause, have failed to find nourishment and have perished in consequence. The realm of Osiris had to be cleared of such beings, and the gods whose duty it was to protect him destroyed them with fire. We may note, too, that in this Division the shadows and souls of the dead were supposed to wander about, and though we do not know how they arrived there, or exactly why they failed to please Osiris, it is quite certain that they were regarded as a danger to the god, and destroyed in consequence.

On the left of Ȧfu-Rā stands a row of deities (vol. i., p. 50 ff.), some wholly in animal forms, who appear to have taken part in the burial ceremonies which were performed for Osiris; the exact functions of many of them are unknown, and the names of certain of them are not found elsewhere. According to the text these gods are clothed with their own bodies of flesh, and their souls speak from them, and their shadows are joined to them. Having been addressed by Ȧfu-Rā they sing praises to the god, and when he has passed from their Division they, as well as the gods on the right of the BOAT, lift up their voices and weep. In return for the lands which were given them by Osiris, in the possession of which they were confirmed by ÅFU-RĀ, these gods have certain duties to perform, viz., to take vengeance upon the fiend SEBÅ, to make NU to come into being, and to cause Ḥāpi to flow. From this it appears that SEBÅ possessed at times power over NU, that is to say, the great celestial watery mass which was the source of the river NILE in Egypt; to destroy this fiend was all-important, for without water the inhabitants of the Ṭuat could not live, and the cessation of the flow of the NILE would cause the ruin and death of the people of Egypt. It is interesting to note the connexion of the NILE with the chief domain of Osiris, and it is, no doubt, a reminiscence of the period in the history of the god when he was a water-god. A knowledge of the beings in these pictures and of the texts of this DIVISION was considered of very great importance for the deceased, for, knowing *their forms* and their names, he would not be terrified by their "roarings," and would not in his haste to escape from them fall headlong into their pits. In this DIVISION of the Ṭuat we see that ÅFU-RĀ was absolute master, and that he is made to create its inhabitants to serve Osiris, and Khenti-Åmenti, and himself, and to allot to them places to dwell in, and food to keep them alive. When he withdraws his light from them they weep, and sink into a state of inertness to await his return on the following day.

THIRD DIVISION OF THE ṬUAT.

II. THE KINGDOM OF KHENTI-ÅMENTI-OSIRIS ACCORDING TO THE BOOK OF GATES.

Before ÅFU-RĀ can pass into the THIRD DIVISION it is necessary for him to pass through a Gate which is protected by two strong walls, with a passage running between them. This passage is swept by flames of fire which proceed from two uraei; each end of it is guarded by a warder in mummied form, and on the inner side of the inner wall is a company of gods. The Gate is called SEPṬET-UAUAU, and the name of its monster serpent is AQEBI. So soon as the Boat enters the DIVISION or HOUR four of the gods of the region appear, and take it in tow; the god is in the same form as before, and has in no way suffered by his passage through the Gate, because at the word of SA the Gate opened, the flames which swept between the walls ceased, and the warders of the passage and the guardian gods withdrew their opposition. In this DIVISION a serious obstacle had to be overcome. Immediately in the fair way of the course of ÅFU-RĀ is a group of eight gods, called FAIU-NETERU, who bear on their shoulders a long pole-like object, each end of which terminates in a bull's head. This object is intended to represent the long tunnel in the earth, each end of which was guarded by a bull, through which, according to one tradition, the night-Sun passed on his journey from the place of sunset to the place of sunrise. At intervals on the tunnel are seated seven gods called NETERU-ÅMIU, i.e., the "gods who are within," and they are intended to represent the guardians of the seven portions into which the tunnel was divided; the name given to the tunnel is "UÅA-TA," i.e., "Boat of the Earth," but there is no doubt that it originally re-

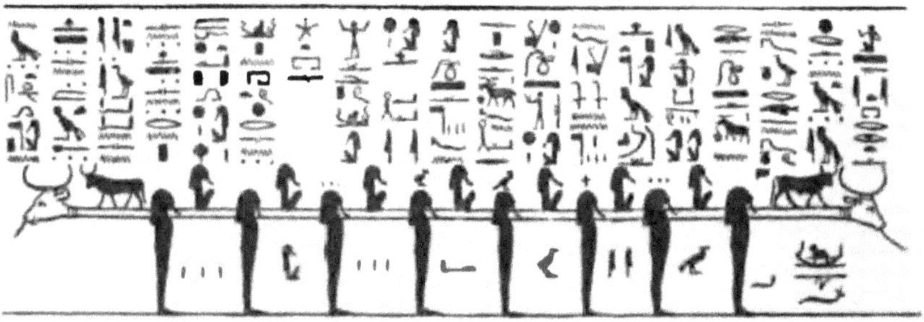

The Boat of the Earth.

presented a kind of Ṭuat which was complete in itself, as the bulls' heads, one at each end of it, prove.

The difficulty of passing through the "Boat of the Earth" is soon overcome, for the gods of the Ṭuat tow ÅFU-RĀ through it, and we see them at the other end of the Division still holding the tow-line in their hands. In front of them are the four gods, whose arms and hands are covered (vol. ii., p. 107), whom we have already seen in the BOOK ÅM-ṬUAT (vol. i., p. 48), where they were in charge of the four boats which filled the picture. It is not difficult to explain why the "Boat of the Earth" was omitted by the Theban priests from their composition; had they kept it in it they would have been obliged to make their god Ȧfu-Rā, the night form of Ȧmen-Rā, to submit to being towed through an inferior Ṭuat, and to being absorbed by the earth-god. The text which refers to this remarkable scene tells us that Āfu-Rā addresses the eight gods who support the "Boat of the Earth," and declares that he who is in it is "holy," and in reply the being or beings Ennurkhata (?) say, "Praised be the Ba," i.e., the ram-headed form of Osiris, which the god has taken, "which the "double bull has swallowed (or, absorbed); let the god "be at peace with that which he hath created." The gods also say, "Praised be Rā, whose Ba hath set him-"self in order with the Earth-god," . Thus it is quite clear that the "Boat of the Earth" is the abode of the "Earth-god."

To the right of Ȧfu-Rā, as he passes through this Division or Hour, are the twelve "holy gods who are in "the Ṭuat," each in his shrine, with its doors thrown wide open; they are guarded by a huge serpent called Seti. These gods are in mummied form, and represent a large class of the beatified dead which exists in the realm of Osiris. According to the text which refers to them Ȧfu-Rā finds the shrines closed when he appears, and the gods within weeping and lamenting; at his word the doors fly open, and the occupants of the shrines obtain air and food and adore him, but when he has passed on the doors of the shrines close again, and the gods betake themselves to lamentations until he reappears on the following night. Thus another class of the dead owes its revivification, light, and food to the beneficence of ÅFU-RĀ rather than to Osiris.

A little beyond the Twelve Shrines is a group of Twelve Gods, who are partially immersed in the "Lake of Boiling Water"; in front of each is a large plant. The waters of this lake have the peculiar property of appearing cool to the taste and touch of the gods who live on it, and who feed upon the plants which grow in it. It is important to notice that the Lake is said to be boiling hot, and that "the birds betake them-"selves to flight when they see the waters thereof, and "when they smell the stench which is in it." Now this description tells us at once that the Lake of Boiling Water is no other than a collection of water which resembles that of the famous "ASPHALTITIS LACUS," or ἀσφαλτῖτις λίμην, which is described by Diodorus Siculus (ii. 48; xix. 98). The water of this Lake is said to be very salt, and of an extremely noxious smell, and the fire which burns beneath the ground, and the stench of the bitumen render the inhabitants of the neighbouring country sickly and short-lived. The country round about is nevertheless well fitted for the cultivation of palms, wherever it is traversed by fresh water. It is quite clear that the author of the Egyptian text cannot have borrowed his description of the Lake from later writers, and it is equally clear that his account of it represents the tradition of the existence of some hot sulphur spring or bituminous lake which existed in Egypt, probably in or near one of the Oases. At Khârga, for example, there are several springs the waters of which reach a temperature of 97° Fahrenheit. As we see in the picture (vol. ii., p. 112) a large plant, or small tree, growing before each of its inhabitants, it is evident that some kind of vegetation flourished in the neighbourhood of the Lake, and the quaint costume of the gods, who, of course, typified the inhabitants of the region, suggests that they were not Egyptian. The dwellers in the LAKE OF BOILING WATER entreat ÅFU-RĀ to come to them, saying, "Send forth thy light "upon us, O thou great god who hast fire in thine eye (vol. ii., p. 113). In answer, the god decrees that their food shall consist of loaves of bread and green herbs, and that their beer shall be made from the *kemtet* plant. This plant has not as yet been accurately identified, but it is tolerably certain that it belonged to a species which was characteristic of the neighbourhood of the Lake.

The beings who stand on the left hand of ÅFU-RĀ are divided into two groups: the first consists of nine men, and the second of nine gods, and each group is under the command of TEMU. Between TEMU and the first company, who are called TCHATCHA we see (vol. ii., p. 114) coiled the monster serpent ĀPEP which has collapsed as a result of the utterance of the word of power by TEMU. This serpent tried to envelop the boat of ÅFU-RĀ with its folds, and then to force a way into his boat; but the TCHATCHA, i.e., "Great Chiefs," cut open its head, and slit its body in many places, and its destruction was finished by TEMU. These TCHATCHA live upon the same food as Rā, but they also partake of the offerings made upon earth to KHENTI-ÅMENTI, the ancient god of the dead of Abydos. The nine gods who follow these are called NEBU-KHERT, and their duty is to repulse the serpents SEBÅ and ÅF (vol. ii., p. 115), and to enchant and to render helpless and motionless ĀPEP when he attempts to force the gates of KHENTI-ÅMENTI. Their food is the same as that of the TCHATCHA, but they possess a power of a remarkable character (which is represented by the words "maāt kheru"), for they know how to utter words in such a way, and with such a tone of voice, that the effect which they wish them to have must of necessity take place. Everything which Osiris possessed as god and judge of the dead he owed to the "*maāt* kheru," or "word of *maāt*." As the god ÅFU-RĀ passes out of the THIRD DIVISION both the TCHATCHA and the NEBU-KHERT give themselves up to lamentation, and they return to the entrance, and wait for the re-appearance of his boat on the following night, when they will again attack SEBÅ, and ÅF, and ĀPEP, and overcome them. The exact place which was set apart for the souls of human beings is nowhere described in the texts.

CHAPTER VIII.

FOURTH DIVISION OF THE ṬUAT.

I. The Kingdom of Seker according to the Book Ȧm-Ṭuat.

The Boat of Ȧfu-Rā has now passed out of the dominions of Khenti-Ȧmenti, the ancient god of the dead of the city of Abydos, and has entered the kingdom of Seker, who is probably the oldest of all the gods of the dead in Egypt. The dominions of Seker were situated in the deserts round about Memphis, and were supposed to cover a large extent of territory, and their characteristics were entirely different from those of the regions ruled over by Khenti-Ȧmenti near Abydos, and from those of the kingdom of Osiris, the lord of Busiris and Mendes, in the Delta. The kingdom of Seker was shrouded in thick darkness, and, instead of consisting of fertile plains and fields, intersected by streams of running water, was formed of bare, barren, sandy deserts, wherein lived monster serpents of terrifying aspect, some having two, and some three heads, and some having wings. This region offered so many difficulties to the passage of the Boat of Ȧfu-Rā, that special means had to be found for overcoming them, and for enabling the god and his followers to proceed northwards to the House of Osiris. As there was no river in the land of SEKER a boat was useless to ÅFU-RĀ, and as the god was unable to travel through the FOURTH DIVISION boldly, and to allow himself to be seen by all the inhabitants thereof, it was arranged that he should pass through a series of narrow corridors, which were provided with doors. The pictures which illustrate the passage of the god through this DIVISION, or HOUR, are arranged in three registers, but the actual corridors through which he travelled are drawn across these obliquely.

The main corridor is called RE-STAU. At the end of the first section of it is the door MĀṬES-SMA-TA (vol. i., p. 63), at the end of the second section is the door MĀṬES-MAU-ĀT (vol. i., p. 71), and at the end of the third section is the door MĀṬES-EN-NEḤEḤ (vol. i., p. 75). An inscription in this last tells us that it is the road by which the body of SEKER enters and that his form is neither seen nor perceived; hence it is clear that the road by which ÅFU-RĀ passed through this DIVISION was supposed to be high up above the dominions of SEKER, and that he never saw that god at all. The name given to this DIVISION, or "CIRCLE," as it is called in the Summary, is ĀNKHET-KHEPERU, and that of its Gate is ÅMENT-SETHAU, ; the goddess of the Hour is called URT-EM-SEKHEMU-S. We may now consider the means employed by ÅFU-RĀ for passing through this HOUR. Looking at the middle register (vol. i., p. 63) we see that the god has discarded his ordinary boat, and that he and his crew are standing in a boat which is formed of a two-headed serpent; a serpent was the best means of transport for the god, because it could glide easily along the sandy floor of the rocky corridor. From the "mouth of the boat," which is drawn by four gods, rays of light are emitted; this light is not strong enough to enable ÅFU-RĀ to see the beings who are on each side of him (vol. i., p. 66), but knowing they are there, he cries out to them, and they hear him. The hidden gods who march in front of the boat are few in number, and the names of many of them are unfamiliar; some of them are connected with Osiris, and all of them are under the control of ÅNPU, or ANUBIS, and perform some act which helps the boat along. Among them may be specially noted Thoth and Horus, above whose outstretched hands is the Eye 𓂀, which is here identified with SEKRI (vol. i., p. 75).

As ÅFU-RĀ journeys on his way there are on his right three serpents, a scorpion, a uraeus serpent, a three-headed serpent with wings and human legs, a few of the gods of the HOUR, a serpent with two necks and heads proceeding from one body, and a tail which terminates in another head (vol. i., pp. 67, 71, 75, 79). On his left are a few more gods and goddesses, the serpents ḤETCH-NĀU, ÅMEN, ḤEKENT, and the terrible three-headed serpent MENMENUT, the face of which illumines the chamber in which KHEPERÅ is born daily (vol. i.,

p. 79). Over the back of the last-named serpent are fourteen heads, which, as M. Maspero has well shown, represent the gods of the first fourteen days of the month, and they are being carried by the serpent to fill the EYE which THOTH and HORUS are bringing through RE-STAU. The beings to the right and left of ȦFU-RĀ are ancient gods of the kingdom of SEKER, and each guards some door or corridor in it which leads to the hidden chamber of SEKER himself.

FIFTH DIVISION OF THE ṬUAT.

I. THE KINGDOM OF SEKER ACCORDING TO THE BOOK ȦM-ṬUAT.

This DIVISION, or HOUR, or CIRCLE, as it is described in the text, is called ȦMENT, and it contains the secret ways, and the doors of the hidden chamber of the holy place of the Land of SEKER, and his flesh, and his members, and his body, in the forms which they had in primeval times; the main gate is called ĀḤĀ-NETERU, the gods are called BAIU-ȦMMIU-ṬUAT, and the goddess of the HOUR is SEMIT-ḤER-ȦBT-UȦA-S. The Boat of ȦFU-RĀ is towed by seven gods and seven goddesses, and is preceded by a few gods who are led by Isis (vol. i., pp. 87, 91, 95, 99, 103, 107, 111); the texts make it clear that ȦFU-RĀ continues his journey by the help of KHEPERȦ. The corridor of RE-STAU through which he travels now bends upwards, and passing by the secret abode of SEKER, by which it is hidden, once more descends to its former level. The Land of Seker is in the form of an elongated ellipse, and is enclosed by a wall of sand; it rests upon the backs of two man-headed sphinxes, each of which is called ÅF and lives upon the voice, or word, of the great god. The duty of these is to guard the Image of Seker. The form in which this god is depicted is that of a hawk-headed man, who stands between a pair of wings that project from the back of a huge serpent having two heads and necks, and a tail terminating in a bearded human head. The Land of Seker is covered by a pyramid having its apex in the form of the head of a goddess, and above it is the vault of night, from which emerges the Beetle of KHEPERÅ. When the Boat of ÅFU-RĀ comes to the pyramid, the Beetle ceases to converse with the goddess of the apex, whose duty it is to pass on its words to SEKER, and betakes itself to the Boat, and begins the revivification of ÅFU-RĀ, who is led on without delay to the end of RE-STAU, where he is received by the MORNING STAR and the light of a new day.

The IMAGE of Seker, which has been described above, lives in thick darkness, and any light which is seen there proceeds from the "eyes of the heads of the "great god whose flesh sendeth forth light," and the god himself lives upon the offerings which are made to the god TEMU upon earth. When ÅFU-RĀ has passed by in his boat there is heard in the Land of

Seker a mighty noise which is like unto that heard in the heights of heaven when they are disturbed by a storm. On one side of the Land of Seker is the serpent TEPȦN (vol. i., p. 95), which presents to the god the offerings made to him daily; on the other is the serpent ĀNKHȦAPAU, which lives upon its own fire, and remains always on guard. Close by are the emblems of the various forms of Seker. Behind the serpent ṬEPȦN is a lake of boiling water, from which project the heads of those who are being boiled therein. This lake or stream is called NETU, , and it is situated in the region of the kingdom of Seker which is called ȦMMĀḤET, ; the unfortunate beings who are in the boiling water weep when the Boat of ȦFU-RĀ has passed them by.

The gods who stand on the other side of the corridor through which ȦFU-RĀ passes are all invoked by him, and they all are assumed to help him on his way, not because they are in duty bound to do so, but because he acknowledged their power by asking their help. Some of them he appealed to because he had created them, but others are manifestly the servants of Seker, and their duty it was to guard his kingdom. A number of them are gods who were set over the waters which lay in the northern part of the DIVISION, and it was all important for ȦFU-RĀ to have their friendly help when he left the back of the serpent and rejoined his own boat. In one portion of the region to the left of ȦFU-

RĀ we see the ḤETEP-NETERU, i.e., a company of eight gods, and the goddess QEṬET-ṬENT; the work of these gods is to be present at the destruction of the dead in the Ṭuat, and to consume their bodies by the flames which they emit from their mouths, and the goddess lives partly on the blood of the dead, and partly on what the gods give her. These gods are provided with blocks on which they cut in pieces the dead, and when they are not thus employed they sing hymns to their god, to the accompaniment of the shaking of sistra; they exist by virtue of the word of power which they have received, and their souls have been given to them (vol. i., p. 110). The dead who are here referred to are those who have succeeded in entering the dread realm of Seker, but who, for want of the influence over the gods there, which could only be obtained by sacrifices and offerings made upon earth, and by the knowledge of mighty words of power, were unable to proceed to the abode of Seker.

When they arrived in the ȦMMĀḤET, some of them were cast into a lake of liquid fire, or of boiling water, and others were first cut in pieces, and then consumed by fire. Thus there is no doubt that there was a hell of fire in the kingdom of Seker, and that the tortures of mutilation and destruction by fire were believed to be reserved for the wicked. Of the rewards of the righteous in this kingdom we have no knowledge whatsoever, and it seems as if the scheme of the Other World of Seker made no provision for the beatified dead; at all events, it provided for them no fertile fields like the Sekhet-Ḥetepet of Osiris, and no Boat of Millions of Years wherein as beings of light they could travel in the company of the Sun-god for ever. The religion of Seker proclaimed that the god lived in impenetrable darkness, in a region of sand, closely guarded by terrible monster serpents, and it had little in it to induce the worshippers of the god to wish to be with him after their departure from this world. The cult of SEKER is one of the oldest in Egypt, and in its earliest form it, no doubt, represents the belief as to the future life of some of the most primitive inhabitants of the country; in fact, it must have originated at a period when some influential body of priests taught that death was the end of all things, and when snakes and bulls were the commonest forms under which the gods of the neighbourhood of Memphis were worshipped. The oldest presentment of the Land of Seker which we have is, of course, not older than the XVIIIth or XIXth Dynasty, and it must be remembered that it is the work of the priests of Thebes, who would be certain to remove any texts, figures, or details which they found inconvenient for their views. It is tolerably certain that the form in which they depicted it is much shorter than that in which it existed originally, and that the attributes and duties of many of the gods have been changed to suit the necessities of the cults of Osiris and Åmen-Rā. Such changes have resulted in great confusion, and at the present time it is impossible to reduce these most interesting, but at the same time most difficult, scenes and texts to their original forms. The priests of Åmen-Rā found it to be impossible to ignore entirely SEKER and his Land, when they were depicting the various Underworlds of Egypt, but it is very suggestive that they make the path of ÅFU-RĀ to be *over* and not *through* his kingdom, and that ÅFU-RĀ had to go on his way without entering the pyramid beneath which reposed the IMAGE of SEKER in the deepest darkness of night, in fact without seeing SEKER at all. On the other hand, they attached the greatest importance to the knowledge of the pictures of the FOURTH and FIFTH DIVISIONS, and they believed that it would enable the body of a man to rejoin his soul, and prevent the goddess KHEMIT, , from hacking it in pieces, and would secure for the believer a share of the offerings made to Seker.

CHAPTER IX.

FOURTH DIVISION OF THE ṬUAT.

II. The Kingdom of Khenti-Åmenti-Osiris according to the Book of Gates.

The pictures and texts of this Division, or Hour, in the Book of Gates vary considerably from those in the Book-Åm-Ṭuat. The god Åfu-Rā appears in his Boat as before with Sa and Ḥekau, and four gods tow him on his way; he has passed through the Gate which is called Nebt-tchefau, and its guardian serpent Tchetbi has in no way resisted his progress. The region now entered by Åfu-Rā has no connexion with the Land of Seker, and it appears to be a continuation of the dominions of Khenti-Åmenti. Immediately in front of the boat are nine sepulchres, each containing a god in mummied form; these are the "gods who are in the following of Osiris, who dwell in their caves" (vol. ii., p. 123). Next come the twelve Hour-goddesses who stand in two groups; between the groups is the monster serpent Ḥereret, which spawns twelve serpents to be consumed by the Twelve Hour-goddesses. As Åfu-Rā goes on his way he adjures the Ṭuat gods to take him to the eastern part of heaven, so that he may visit the habitations of the god ÅRES, (or SÅR) , and when he has come to them, he orders the doors to open, and raises up the beings therein whose "souls are broken," and allots to them meat and drink. The Hour-goddesses are the daughters of Rā, and their work is to guide their father through the night; six of them represent the first six hours of the night, and the other six the last six. These are here (vol. ii., p. 123) depicted together, whilst in the BOOK ÅM-ṬUAT each appears in the boat of ÅFU-RĀ in the Hour to which she belongs.

On the right of ÅFU-RĀ are the Twelve gods who "carry their doubles" (vol. ii., p. 131) and who live upon the offerings which are made to them and upon what is given to them by ṬESERT-BAIU, i.e., the place of holy souls. Their duty is to offer their *kau* or doubles to the god, whom they address as the "lord of years and of everlastingness which hath no diminution" (vol. ii., p. 130). Beyond these gods are two lakes, viz., the LAKE OF LIFE, and the LAKE OF THE LIVING URAEI. Round the LAKE OF LIFE stand twelve jackal-headed gods who invite ÅFU-RĀ to bathe in it, even as the "lord of the gods" did, and who state that the souls of the dead do not come near it because it is holy. When he passes out of this DIVISION they lift up their voices in lamentation (vol. ii., p. 132). The LIVING URAEI turn back the souls from their Lake, and the mere sound of the words which they utter destroys the shadows of the dead who have succeeded in coming near it. They preserve with great care the flames and fire which are in them, so that they may hurl them at the enemies of ÅFU-RĀ.

In the course of his journey through this HOUR ÅFU-RĀ passes the shrine of KHENTI-ÅMENTI, the ancient god of Abydos, which is seen on the left (vol. ii., p. 137); he is in mummied form, wears the white crown, as befits a god of the South, and stands on a serpent. Immediately before the shrine is the Flame-goddess NESERT. Before and behind the shrine are twelve gods, at the head of the first company being ḤERU-UR, or "Horus the Aged." ḤERU-UR addresses the god in the shrine by the names "Osiris" and "Khenti-Åmenti," and declares that he has performed the magical ceremonies which have made KHENTI-ÅMENTI to be the "Governor of the Ṭuat," to such purpose that the spirits of the blessed (*khu*, ) look upon him with awe, and the dead, i.e., the damned, (*mit* ) are in terror of him. Here we have the proof of the existence of the belief that Osiris was enabled to travel safely through the Ṭuat by means of the spells, and incantations, and magical formulae, and words of power which were uttered by ḤERU-UR. The Twelve gods who are in front of the shrine ascribe praise and dominion to KHENTI-ÅMENTI, and declare that his son Horus has restored to him his crown, and crushed his enemies, and made strong OSIRIS-KHENTI-ÅMENTI. To these ÅFU-RĀ makes no answer, but he calls upon Horus to avenge him on those who work against him, and to cast them to the Master of the lords of the pits, so that they may be destroyed. Now the pits here referred to are four in number (vol. ii., p. 137), and they are filled with fire; into these the enemies of the god are cast, and the keepers of them are adjured by Horus to watch and tend the fires. Who the plotters against the god may be it is impossible to say, but it is quite clear that one portion of the FOURTH DIVISION OF THE ȚUAT was a fiery hell wherein all the wicked were consumed. It is interesting to note that of the beings who are to the left of the Boat of ÅFU-RĀ Horus is the only one whom the god addresses.

FIFTH DIVISION OF THE ȚUAT.

II. THE KINGDOM OF KHENTI-ÅMENTI-OSIRIS ACCORDING TO THE BOOK OF GATES.

The FIFTH, like the FOURTH DIVISION of the BOOK OF GATES, in no way resembles that in the BOOK ÅM-ȚUAT, and it has nothing whatsoever to do with the kingdom of SEKER. The god ÅFU-RĀ, having passed through the Gate of the DIVISION or HOUR, which is called ÅRIT, and which has been opened by the monster serpent TEKA-HRÅ that guarded it, is towed along by four of the gods of this section of the

Ṭuat. The ministers of the god consist of nine gods whose hands and arms are covered, and twelve gods who are under the direction of ḤERI-QENBET-F; the nine gods are called KHERU-ENNUTCHI, i.e., "those who hold the serpent ENNUTCHI," and the twelve gods BAIU RETH ÅMMIU ṬUAT, i.e., the "souls of men who dwell in the Ṭuat" (vol. ii., pp. 144, 145). The exact functions of Ennutchi are not known, but his presence is baleful, and ÅFU-RĀ straightway calls upon the group of gods to destroy him; the god would press on to the next Gate, NEBT-ĀḤĀU, but ENNUTCHI can travel to that point, and he must therefore be removed.

The next group of gods is of peculiar interest, for they represent the souls of those who have spoken "what is right and true upon earth, and who have magnified the forms of the god RĀ." In return for such moral rectitude and piety, ÅFU-RĀ orders ḤERI-QENBET-F to invite them to "sit at peace in their habitations in the corner of those who are with myself," where praises shall be sung to their souls, and where they shall have air in abundance to breathe; they shall, moreover, have joints of meat to eat in SEKHET-ÅARU. Besides this, offerings shall be made to them upon earth, even as they are to the god ḤETEPI, the lord of SEKHET-ḤETEPET (vol. ii., pp. 145, 146). Now from these statements some very interesting deductions may be made. In the first place, it is now certain that there was a place specially set apart for the souls of men in the Ṭuat, and that those who were allowed to enter it had lived a life of moral rectitude, and had followed after righteousness and integrity when they were upon earth. Secondly, they were allowed to live in the corner of the SEKHET-ḤETEPET with the great god himself, in the place where, as we know from the Papyrus of Ȧni (see above, p. 44), most wonderful grain grew. Thirdly, an everlasting supply of offerings made upon earth was assured them, and in this respect they were coequal with ḤETEPI, the chief god of the Field of Peace (or, Field of Offerings). Thus the religion of Osiris undoubtedly taught that those who were good on this earth were rewarded in the next world.

On the right of ȦFU-RĀ are the twelve gods called HENIU-ȦMMIU-ṬUAT, i.e., "those who sing praises in the Ṭuat," and the twelve gods called KHERU-ENNUḤU-EM-ṬUAT, i.e., "those who hold the cord in the Ṭuat," and the four ḤENBIU gods (vol. ii., pp. 148-150). The first company of gods are, as we learn from the text, engaged in praising ȦFU-RĀ, and they have been rewarded with the exalted office which they hold in Ȧment because they praised Rā at sunrise and sunset when they lived upon earth, and because Rā was "satisfied" with what they did for him. They enjoy, moreover, a share of the offerings which are made to the god. A little beyond the HENIU are the "gods who hold the measuring cord," and by the orders of the great god they go over the fields of Ȧmentet, and measure and mark out the plots of ground which are to be allotted to the KHU, or spirits of the righteous. Every spirit is judged by the god of law and righteousness, and only after a strict examination is he allowed to take possession of his allotment. As there seems to have been only one standard of moral and religious excellence all the allotments were probably of the same size. The food of the spirits who live in the homesteads which have been thus measured in SEKHET-ÅARU comes from the crops which grow in that region, and the four ḤENBIU gods, who superintended the measuring of the fields, are ordered to provide sand, that is to say soil, for the replenishing of the ground.

The beings who are on the left of ÅFU-RĀ in this Division are not less interesting than those on the right. Among these are are four representatives of the four great classes into which the Egyptians divided mankind, namely, the RETH (for REMTH), the NEḤESU, the THEMEḤU, and the ĀAMU (vol. ii., p. 153). Of these the RETH, i.e., the "men" *par excellence*, were Egyptians, who came into being from the tears which fell from the Eye of RĀ. The THEMEḤU, or Libyans, were also descended from the Eye of RĀ. The ĀAMU were the people of the deserts to the north and east of Egypt, Sinai, etc., and the NEḤESU were the black tribes of Nubia and the Sûdân. It is noteworthy that the members of each nation or people keep together. The representatives of the Four Nations are followed by twelve gods who are called KHERU-ĀḤĀU-ÅMENT, i.e., "The Holders of the Time of Life in Åment," and who hold the serpent METERUI. These remarkable beings have in their hands the power to determine the length of life which is to be meted out to the souls who have been doomed to destruction in Åmenti, that is to say, they were able to defer the doom which had been decreed for souls, though in the end they were compelled to carry out the edict of destruction. In close connexion with these gods are the TCHATCHAU, or "Great Chiefs," who were believed to write the edicts of destruction against the damned (vol. ii., p. 156), and to record the duration of the lives of those who were in Åmentet; in fact, they appear to have kept the registers of Osiris, and to have served in some respects as recording angels. From what has been said above it will be clear that all the scenes and texts which illustrate and describe the Kingdom of Seker have been omitted from the BOOK OF GATES, and that the first five sections of this work describe—1. The Antechamber of the Ṭuat. 2. The Divisions of the Kingdom of KHENTI-ÅMENTI, which extended from Abydos to a region a little to the north of Memphis. We may now proceed to consider the Kingdom of Osiris, the lord of Mendes and Busiris.

CHAPTER X.

SIXTH DIVISION OF THE ṬUAT.

I. Kingdom of Osiris according to the Book Am-Ṭuat.

This Division, or Hour, is the first of four which are devoted to the Kingdom of Osiris; its name is Metchet-mu-nebt-Ṭuat, its Gate is called Sepṭ-Metu, and the Hour-goddess is Mesperit-Ȧr-Āt-maātu. Here we see at once that the god Ȧfu-Rā has re-entered his boat, and that he has discarded the serpent-boat in which he travelled through the Land of Seker; the boat advances by means of paddling and not by towing. The greater part of the road of Ȧfu-Rā in this Division is occupied by a very long building—or series of houses, or chambers, set close together—which contains the forms of Osiris. Here are four representatives of each of four classes of beings, viz., the Suteniu, or kings of Upper Egypt, the Bȧtiu, or kings of Lower Egypt, the Ḥeteptiu, or those who have been abundantly supplied with offerings, and the Khu, or spirits of the beatified dead. Thus it seems that the first mansion of the House of Osiris contains royal folk, the rich, and the superlatively good (vol. i., p. 117-120); as Ȧfu-Rā passes these by he salutes them, and wishes them an abundant supply of offerings, and entreats them to hack ĀPEP in pieces for him. Immediately beyond these we see represented the transformation of ÅFU-RĀ into the living Sun-god. Here is the five-headed serpent ĀSHT-ḤRÅU, and on his back lies the dead Sun-god; with his right hand, which is raised above his head, he is drawing to himself the Beetle of KHEPERÅ, which is the type of regeneration,

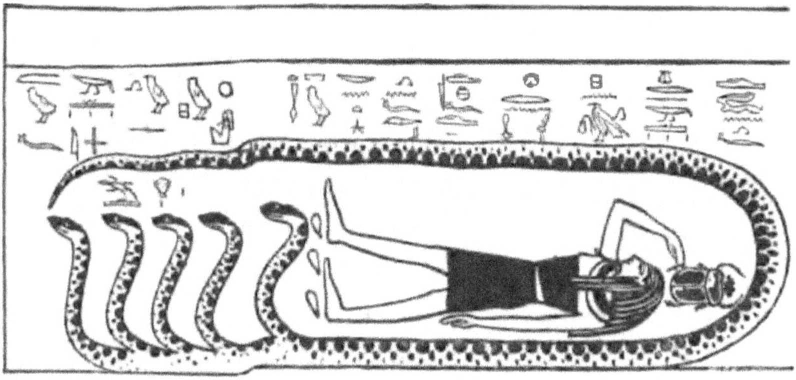

The Serpent Āsht-ḥrâu.

or new birth, or resurrection. This is the equivalent of the scene in the BOOK ÅM-ṬUAT where the Beetle descends from the vault of night, and joining itself to the Boat of ÅFU-RĀ revivifies the dead Sun-god (see vol. i., p. 103). That this revivification of ÅFU-RĀ should take place at the end of the SIXTH DIVISION is quite correct, for at this point the god arrives at the most northerly limit of his course. He has travelled due north from Thebes and Abydos, and has occupied six hours in performing the journey; he must now alter his course and travel towards the East so that he may appear at BAKHAU, , the Mountain of Sunrise. The path over which he now journeys is called the "secret path of Åmentet," and he who knoweth it, and the names of those who are on it, and their forms, shall partake of the offerings made to the gods of Osiris, and receive the gifts which his relatives (, *ābt*)[1] shall make upon earth.

On the right of ÅFU-RĀ are a company of gods and goddesses, and a group of sceptres surmounted by crowns and uraei, and provided with knives; these are the beings who hold and cultivate the territory in this DIVISION, or HOUR, and minister to the wants of the followers of Osiris. Beyond these we have a lion, the two Eyes of Horus, three deities, and three small sepulchres, into each of which, through an opening under the roof, a serpent is belching fire (vol. i., pp. 124-130). In each sepulchre is an "image" of Rā, i.e., a human head, a hawk's wing, and a hind-quarter of a lion, and these appear to be symbols under which the god was worshipped in and around Ånnu, or Heliopolis. On the left of ÅFU-RĀ are eight gods and four goddesses, whose duty it is to accompany his Boat, and to escort the souls and shadows of men through the Division, and to provide the spirits with food and water. Next is the

[1] See above, p. 66.

monster serpent "Am-Khu," i.e., "Eater of the Spirits," whose duty it is to devour the shadows of the dead, and to eat up the spirits of the foes of Rā; from his back spring the heads of the Four Children of Horus, and they come into being when they hear the voice of Åfu-Rā. Beyond these are four Osiris forms, "which stand though they are seated, and move though they are motionless," and nine serpents armed with knives, which represent the ancient gods, Ta-thenen, Temu, Kheperȧ, Shu, Seb, Åsȧr (Osiris), Ḥeru, Åpu, and Ḥetepui. These gods had faces of fire, and lived in the water of Tathenen, and they only came to life by virtue of the words of power of Åfu-Rā, who is now to be regarded as Kheperȧ.

SEVENTH DIVISION OF THE ṬUAT.

I. Kingdom of Osiris according to the Book Åm-Ṭuat.

The name of this Division, or Hour, is Thepḥet-shetat, the name of the Gate is Ruti-Åsȧr, and the goddess of the Hour is Kheftes-Hȧu-ḥesq-Neḥa-ḥrȧ. On looking at the "secret path of Åmentet" wherein Åfu-Rā is still travelling, we note that the face of the god is turned in another direction, that the crew is increased by Isis and by Ser, , whose name has also been read Semsu, and that the canopy under which Åfu-Rā stands is formed of the body of the serpent

Meḥen (vol. i., p. 140). There is a good reason for these changes, for the god has now to traverse a region where there is not sufficient water to float his boat or to permit of its being towed; moreover, his way is blocked by a monster serpent called Neḥa-ḥrȧ, which lies on a sand bank 450 cubits long.[1] In other words, the Boat of Ȧfu-Rā has arrived at a region of sand-banks and shallows, where serpents and crocodiles live; but the words of power of Isis, the great sorceress, and of Ser, and of the god himself protect him from mishap, and eventually he passes through this division by taking upon himself the form of the serpent Meḥen in which he glides onwards. The region of the Ṭuat where the serpent Āpep or Neḥa-ḥrȧ lives is called Tchau, , and it is 440 cubits long, and 440 cubits wide; his head and his tail are caught in fetters by Serqet and Ḥer-ṭesu-f respectively, and these gods have transfixed him to the ground with six huge knives (vol. i., p. 142). When the body of the serpent has been removed, Ȧfu-Rā advances, and, passing four goddesses each armed with a knife, arrives at four rectangular buildings. Inside each building (vol. i., p. 144) is a mound of sand, and at each end of each building is the head of a man. These buildings are the tombs wherein the four chief forms of the Sun-god have been buried, the first containing the "Form of Tem," the second the "Form of Kheperȧ," the third

[1] This statement is found in the Summary.

the "Form of RĀ," and the fourth the "Form of OSIRIS." The heads which appear at the ends of the tombs are those of the enemies who were slain at the tombs, and were buried in the foundations in order to drive away evil spirits. The texts which refer to these scenes state that the four goddesses join in slaying ĀPEP, that the human heads appear as soon as any one comes to the tombs; and that as soon as they have heard the voice of ÅFU-RĀ, and he has gone by, they "eat their own forms," i.e., they disappear until Rā again comes (vol. i., p. 145).

On the right of the Boat of ÅFU-RĀ, and facing it, are HORUS, and the twelve gods of the hours, who protect the tombs of Osiris, and assist RĀ in his journey (vol. i., pp. 154-156); next come twelve goddesses of the hours, who face in the opposite direction, and are entreated to guide "the god who is on "the horizon to the beautiful Åmentet in peace." Beyond these is the great Crocodile, called ĀBSHE-ÅM-ṬUAT, which is stretched out at full length over the tomb of Osiris; as the Boat of ÅFU-RĀ passes it, the god addresses words to Osiris, who for a season puts forth his head, which disappears as soon as the Boat has entered the next DIVISION.

On the left of ÅFU-RĀ we have also a number of gods and goddesses who belong to this DIVISION, and among them may be specially noticed the serpent MEḤEN, the lord of this region; his body is bent in the form of a canopy, and beneath is the "Flesh of Osiris" in the form of a god (ÅFU-ÅSAR) seated on a throne (vol. i., p. 149). In front of it are a number of the enemies of Osiris, some decapitated by the LYNX-GODDESS, and some in fetters which are held in the hands of the god ÅNKU (vol. i., pp. 149, 150). Beyond these are three living souls, representatives of the blessed dead in this region, and the "Flesh of Tem" (ÅFU-TEM) in the form of a god seated on the back of a huge serpent resembling MEḤEN (vol. i., p. 151).

EIGHTH DIVISION OF THE ṬUAT.

I. KINGDOM OF OSIRIS ACCORDING TO THE BOOK ÅM-ṬUAT.

The name of this DIVISION, or HOUR, or CITY, is ṬEBAT-NETERU-S, its Gate is called ĀḤĀ-ÅN-URṬ-NEF, and its Hour-goddess is NEBT-USHAU. The Boat of ÅFU-RĀ now enters one of the most holy places in the Kingdom of Osiris, for in it abide the Four Forms of TATHENEN. Looking at the Boat (vol. i., p. 164) we see that ISIS and SER are no longer in it, a fact which indicates that the dangers incidental to passing through this DIVISION are not great, and that it is towed by a company of gods. Immediately in front of them are nine SHEMSU, or "Followers," i.e., "servants" (of Osiris), each with an object before him (vol. i., p. 167), which indicates that he is a properly bandaged mummy, and leading these are Four Rams, each wearing a different kind of crown, which represent the Four Forms of TATHENEN (vol. i., pp. 168, 169). The heads which are attached to the symbols of the "Followers" only appear when they hear the voice of ÅFU-RĀ, and when he has passed them they disappear; the huge knives which they have are used in slaughtering any of the enemies of Rā who may succeed in entering the City.

On the right and left of the path of ÅFU-RĀ are a number of "Circles" in which dwell the "gods" who have been mummified, and for whom all the prescribed rites and ceremonies have been performed; the greater number of these gods are not well known, and their exact functions are not well understood. The CIRCLES on the right are: 1. ḤETEPET-NEB-S, 2. ḤETEMET-KHEMIU, 3. ḤAPSEMU-S, 4. SEḤERT-BAIU-S, 5. ĀAT-SETEKAU, 6. The door ṬES-AMEM-MIT-EM-SHETA-F. As ÅFU-RĀ passes these gods their doors fly open and those within hear what he says, and they respond with cries which are like unto those of male cats, or the "noise of the confused murmur of the living," or the "sound of those who go down to the battle-field of Nu," or the "sound of the cry of the Divine Hawk of Horus," or the "twittering of the birds in a nest of water-fowl." The CIRCLES on the left are: 1. SESHETA, 2. ṬUAT, 3. ÅS-NETERU, 4. ÅAKEBI, 5. NEBT-SEMU-NIFU, 6. The door ṬES-KHAIBITU-ṬUATIU. The sounds made by the gods in these resemble the "hum of many honey-bees," the "sound of the swathed ones," the "sound of men who lament," the sounds "of bulls and other male animals," and the sound of those "who make supplication through terror" (vol. i., pp. 170 ff.).

NINTH DIVISION OF THE ṬUAT.

I. KINGDOM OF OSIRIS ACCORDING TO THE BOOK ÀM-ṬUAT.

The name of this DIVISION, or HOUR, or CITY, is BEST-ÀRU-ĀNKHET-KHEPERU, the Gate is called SAA-EM-ḲEB, and its Hour-goddess is ṬUATET-MĀKETET-EN-NEB-S. The Boat of ÀFU-RĀ now enters the last of the four DIVISIONS of the Kingdom of Osiris, and moves without the aid of towing. Immediately in front of it are twelve sailor-gods, each grasping a short paddle with both hands; they appear to have been depicted in front of the Boat because there was no room for them in it. The god is still under the form of MEḤEN, and is still passing over the secret path of ÀMENTET, and his Sailors sing to him, and as they do so they scatter water from the stream with their paddles on the Spirits who dwell in this City (vol. i., pp. 189-191). In front of these are three deities, seated on baskets, and the god ḤETEP-NETERU-ṬUAT; they accompany the Boat of ÀFU-RĀ, and it is their duty to provide food, or offerings, for the gods who are in the DIVISION. On the right of the path of the god are twelve uraei, who lighten the darkness by means of the fire which they pour out from their mouths: they rest upon objects which suggest that they have received their places in this DIVISION because all the appointed funeral rites and ceremonies were duly performed for them (vol. i., p. 201). In front of these are the nine gods who represent the field-labourers in the Ṭuat (vol. i., pp. 204, 205), and each holds a heavy stick, similar to that which the peasants in Egypt have always carried to protect themselves. Their "ganger" is ḤERU-ḤER-SHE-ṬUAT, i.e., "He who is over the lakes (or sand) in the Ṭuat."

On the left of the path of the god are twelve gods, each of whom is seated on a weaving instrument (vol. i., p. 195), and twelve goddesses (vol. i., p. 199); the gods are the TCHATCHA, or "Great Chiefs" of Osiris, and their duty is to avenge Osiris each day, and to overthrow the enemies of Osiris, and the goddesses spring into existence when they hear the god's voice, and sing praises to Osiris each day.

CHAPTER XI.

SIXTH DIVISION OF THE ṬUAT.

II. Kingdom of Osiris according to the Book of Gates.

The Boat of Ȧfu-Rā, having passed through the first five Divisions of the Ṭuat, now, according to the Book of Gates, arrives near the southern part of the Delta, and near the kingdom of Osiris, lord of Mendes and Busiris. Before, however, the god can enter it, he must pass through the Gate of the Sixth Division, which is called Nebt-Āḥā, and which is guarded by the monster serpent Set-em-maat-f. In the Gate or close to it, is the Judgment Hall of Osiris, and it is tolerably certain that no soul entered his kingdom without being weighed in the balance of the god. The scene in which the Hall is depicted is of great interest, for it is different in many important particulars from the representations of the Judgment which we find on papyri, even in those which belong to the period of the XVIIIth and XIXth Dynasties. All the texts which describe it are written in hieroglyphics, but in many of them the hieroglyphics have, as Champollion pointed

Nebseni being weighed against his heart.

out, special and very unusual values, and the title "enigmatic writing" given to them by Goodwin is appropriate. In the ordinary Judgment Scenes we find that the heart of the deceased is weighed in the balance against the feather symbolic of Maāt or righteousness, that the operation of weighing is carried out by Thoth and Anubis in the presence of the great gods, the owner of the heart himself sometimes looking on, that the gods accept and ratify the verdict of Thoth, and that the deceased is then led into the presence of Osiris by Horus. Sometimes the heart of the deceased is weighed against his whole body, as in the Papyrus of Nebseni, and at other times the pans of the scales only contain weights. In the scene before us the arrangement is quite different. Osiris is seated on a chair of state, and wears the crowns of the South and North united; in

The Scales of Osiris, with weights.

his hands are the symbols of "life," 𓋹, and "rule," 𓋾. His chair stands on a raised platform, on the nine steps of which stand the nine gods who form his company; beneath the feet of the god, perhaps under his platform, are the dead, i.e., the damned, or his enemies. The top of the Hall is protected with a row of spear heads, and from the ceiling hang four heads of gazelle, or oryges; according to a legend certain enemies of Osiris transformed themselves into these animals, and were slain by the god. On the platform, immediately in front of the god, stands THOTH, in the form of a mummy, and he serves as the standard of the balance; the object in the pan is being weighed against the symbol of "evil," 𓅪, which it seems to counterbalance exactly. This being so, it seems that the wickedness of the deceased did not go beyond a recognized limit. ANUBIS, in the upper corner of the scene, addresses some words to THOTH, who bears the Balance on his shoulders. In the small boat near the Balance is a pig being beaten by an ape;[1] the name of the pig is ĀM-Ā, but neither his functions, nor those of the ape are clearly known. The ape may be the equivalent of the dog-headed ape which sits on the beam of the Balance in the pictures in the Theban papyri, and the pig may represent the Eater of the Dead; but at present these are matters of conjecture. With reference to the pig it is interesting to note that

[1] The boat sometimes contains two apes (see Sharpe, *Eg. Inscriptions*, part ii., pl. 9), and in a tomb at Thebes one ape is in the boat and one outside it (see the illustration opposite).

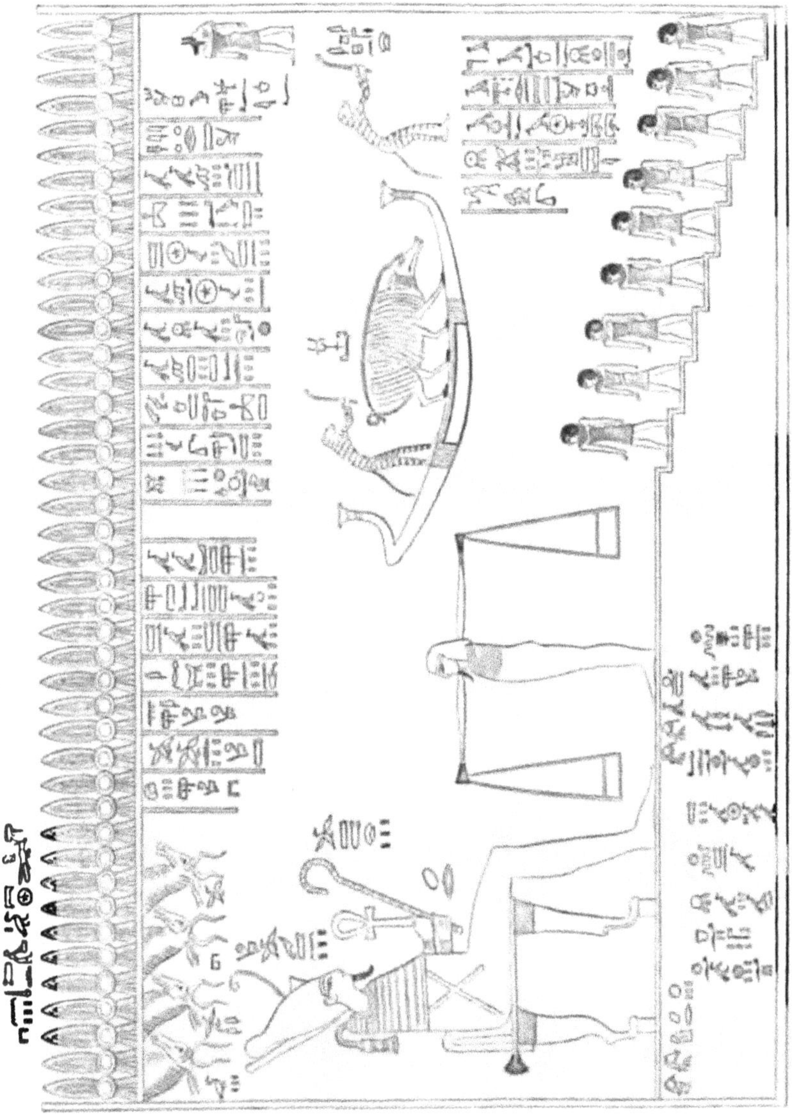

The Judgment Hall of Osiris according to the Book of Gates. (From Champollion, *Monuments de l'Égypte*, tom. iii., pl. cclxxii.)

in the Papyrus of Nekht the deceased is seen grasping a chain by which a serpent is fettered, and spearing a pig. The chief point of interest in the whole scene is the fact that the Judgment here depicted is of a more primitive character than that given in the Book of the Dead.

The Boat of ȦFU-RĀ, having passed through or by the Hall of Osiris, now enters the abode of the blessed, and the pictures of the SIXTH DIVISION are intended to show us the occupations of those who have been declared to be "right and true." The Boat is towed through this DIVISION by four gods of the Ṭuat and immediately in front of it is a series of jackal-headed sceptres of SEB, to each of which two enemies are tied; by the side of each sceptre is a god, who takes care that the punishments which have been decreed by Osiris are duly executed. It is noteworthy that the two eyes of Rā, 𓂀𓂀, are placed between the first two sceptres (vol. ii., p. 172). The Egyptian text (vol. ii., p. 183) makes it quite clear that the enemies of Osiris are tied to the standards of SEB according to the god's decree, and preparatory to slaughter in the Hall of Rā.

Nekht spearing the pig of evil.

To the right of the path of ȦFU-RĀ are twelve MAĀTI gods who carry MAĀT, and twelve ḤETEPTIU gods who carry provisions. These are they who offered up incense to the gods, and whose *kau* or "doubles have been washed clean, whose iniquities have been done away, and who were right in the judgment." Therefore has Osiris decreed them to be "Maāt of Maāt," i.e., most "righteous," and he has given them a place of abode in his own presence with peace and the food of Maāt thereon to live (vol. ii., pp. 177, 186).

To the left of the path of ȦFU-Rā are twelve gods, each of whom is tending a colossal ear of wheat, and twelve gods provided with sickles, engaged in reaping. The ears of wheat here growing are the "members of Osiris," (*ḥāt Sar,* ), that is, they are regarded as parts of the god's own body,[1] and the inhabitants of the Kingdom of Osiris and human beings on earth alike ate the body of the god when they ate bread of wheat. The wheat which grew in the kingdom of Osiris was, of course, larger, and finer in every respect than that which grew on earth, and it is expressly said that the "Khu," i.e., beatified spirits, feed upon the divine grain (NEPRȦ) in the land of the Light-god (vol. ii., p. 188). Therefore since the divine grain is here a form of Osiris, the Khu live upon the god himself, and eat him daily; this is exactly the kind of belief which we should expect the primitive Egyptians at one period to possess. The idea of a heaven wherein

[1] Prof. Wiedemann has collected a number of important facts on this subject in his most interesting paper "OSIRIS VÉGÉTANT."

wheat grew luxuriantly, and food made of the same could be had in abundance, was evolved in their mind after the introduction of wheat into Egypt from Asia, and after the Egyptians had settled down to agricultural pursuits. The god of such a heaven was naturally the Corn-god NEPRÀ, but it seems as if Osiris were identified with him at a very early period, and as if, finally, he absorbed all his attributes. The idea of a heaven of this simple character must of necessity be very old, and it presupposes the existence of beliefs concerning the future life which the later Egyptians must often in their secret hearts have repudiated. In the BOOK OF GATES we find NEB-ĀUT-ÀB, i.e., RĀ, decreeing that the wheat of this region should germinate, and that the plants should grow to a large size, and those who are tending the crops beseech him to shine upon them, for when he shines the grain sprouts and the plants grow.

Now, though Osiris was from a material point of view the Grain-god, or Corn-god, and the wheat was his members, which were eaten by his followers, he was also the lord of MAĀT, i.e., "righteousness" and "integrity," and even the personification of those abstract qualities. When, addressing the MAĀTI gods, he declares they are "MAĀT OF MAĀT," he makes it clear that he considers them to be beings of like nature to himself, and that they will live upon MAĀT; in other words, they have become Truth, and they will live upon Truth, and exist as Truth for ever. The MAĀTI gods apparently represent the highest conception of spiritual beings which the Egyptians arrived at in the early period, and which is only paralleled by that of a later period, according to which the followers of the Sun-god, who travelled with him in the Boat of Millions of Years, eventually became beings consisting of nothing but light. It would be useless to contend that either conception was believed in throughout the country generally, for the Egyptians as a nation believed in a heaven wherein happiness of a very material character was to be found; still there must have been among the educated and priestly classes devout men and women whose yearnings for future happiness would not be satisfied with promises of cakes, and ale, and love-making, and to whom the idea of becoming the counterpart of the eternal god of the dead would afford consolation and hope.

SEVENTH DIVISION OF THE ṬUAT.

II. KINGDOM OF OSIRIS ACCORDING TO THE BOOK OF GATES.

The SEVENTH DIVISION, or HOUR, is entered by the Gate PESṬIT, which is guarded by a monster serpent called ÅKHA-EN-MAAT; the pictures and texts are incomplete on the sarcophagus of Seti I., and those which are given in vol. ii., p. 190 ff., are taken from M. E. Lefébure's *Les Hypogées Royaux de Thèbes*, tom. ii., part ii., pl. 11 ff. The Boat of ÅFU-RĀ is, as before, towed by four gods of the Ṭuat. The procession of the ministers of the god consists of twenty-four gods, twelve of whom have their hands and arms hidden; these last "are invisible beings, but those who are in the Ṭuat and the dead can see them," and Rā promises them that they shall be with him in Ḥet-Benben, that is to say, in the heavenly counterpart of one of the temples of the Sun-god of Heliopolis (see vol. ii., p. 194 ff.).

To the right of the path of Ȧfu-Rā are twelve gods armed with clubs having forked ends; they are called Kheru-metauḥ, and their duty is to repulse the serpent Āpep. Immediately in front of them is the serpent Sebȧ, on the head and back of which twelve human heads are seen; these make their appearance (vol. ii., p. 206 ff.) at the coming of Ȧfu-Rā, and the twelve gods who grasp the monster's body are exhorted to destroy them. The serpent is called Sebȧ, and Āpep, and Ḥefau. Beyond these groups of gods are twelve star-gods, who hold in their hands a long rope which is twisted round the neck of a god in mummied form called Qān, or Āqen, or Nāq (vol. ii., pp. 208, 209). To the left of the path of Ȧfu-Rā is the god of the Ṭuat, called Ṭuati, who leans on a staff, and is in charge of the twelve mummies which lie on the back of the serpent Nehep; the serpent has twenty-four lions' legs arranged at intervals (vol. ii., p. 210), and a mummy rests over each pair of them. The mummies are described as "those who are in inertness," and "those who are in the body of Osiris asleep."

As ÅFU-RĀ passes them the god ṬUATI encourages them to loosen their bandages, to untie and take off their wigs, to collect their bones, to gather together their flesh and their members, to open their eyes and look at the light, to get up from their state of inertness, and to take possession of their fields in SEKHET-NEBT-ḤETEPET. Beyond these is another group of gods whose duty it is to live near the pool of a serpent, the water of which is of fire; its flames proceed from the serpent, and they are so fierce that the gods and souls of the earth dare not approach them. On the other hand, the gods of the pool are adjured to give water to KHENTI-ÅUḲERT, i.e., the Governor of Åuḳert. Now Åuḳert is the name of the Other World, or Ṭuat, of HELIOPOLIS, and the mention of it and of ḤET-BENBEN suggests that the Kingdom of Osiris according to the BOOK OF GATES was made to include that of the god TEMU, a form of the Night-sun. The gods who sit round the lake of fire receive their bodies and souls from the serpent NEHEP, and then they journey into SEKHET-ÅARU, which apparently has not yet been reached.

EIGHTH DIVISION OF THE ṬUAT.

II. KINGDOM OF OSIRIS ACCORDING TO THE BOOK OF GATES.

The Boat of ÅFU-RĀ next passes through the Gate of Bekhkhi, which is guarded by the monster serpent

SET-ḤRȦ, and is towed over this DIVISION, or HOUR, by the gods of the Ṭuat. The region is a remarkable one, and it certainly forms part of the Kingdom of the Sun-god of ȦNNU, or Heliopolis. At one end of the long Lake, or Pool, which represents the celestial waters of NU (vol. ii., pp. 225, 226) stands the god "who dwelleth in NU," and in the Lake itself we see four groups of beings in human forms who are called "Bathers" (Herpiu), "Floaters" (Ȧḳiu), "Swimmers" (Nubiu), and "Divers" (Khepau). The gods who tow the Boat call on the dwellers in this DIVISION to praise the soul of RĀ, which is in heaven, and his body, which is on earth; for heaven is made young again by his soul, and earth by his body. Then, addressing the god in the Boat, they declare that they will make his paths straight in ȦḲERT, and that they will make his Boat to pass over the beings who are immersed in the waters of the Lake. The god "who dwelleth in NU" then calls upon the beings in the water to pay homage to RĀ, and he promises that they shall enjoy breath for their nostrils, and peace in their cisterns of water. Their souls, which are upon earth, shall enjoy offerings in abundance and shall never die, and shall be as fully provided with food as is RĀ, whose body is on earth, but whose soul is in heaven.

On the left of the path of ȦFU-RĀ are twelve TCHATCHA, or "Great Chiefs," and nine SOULS, who are adoring a god (vol. ii., pp. 227, 231); before each Soul are a loaf of bread and some *sekemu* herbs. The TCHATCHA perform a very important duty in this DIVISION, for they distribute to the SOULS who have been ordered by RĀ to live by the fiery Lake SERSER the food which has been allotted to them; in other words, they give the SOULS the portion of food which it has been decreed they should receive daily, and no more and no less, and the SOULS receive their destined allowance, and have to be content therewith. Judging from the texts here and elsewhere in the BOOK OF GATES it seems that there was some power in the Ṭuat, probably KHENTI-ÅMENTI, or OSIRIS KHENTI-ÅMENTI, who decreed that the beings therein should receive a regular, fixed, and unalterable allowance of food each day, and who appointed ministers, who are here called TCHATCHA, to see that each being received his "ration," without addition, and without diminution. The Sun-god in passing through the Ṭuat confirms the "ration," and orders its continuance to each being therein.

On the right of the path of ÅFU-RĀ is HORUS THE AGED, leaning on a staff, and addressing a company of twelve of the enemies of Osiris (vol. ii., pp. 232-234), who stand with their arms tied together behind their backs in very painful attitudes. Before these is a huge serpent called KHETI, belching fire into the faces of the enemies of Osiris; in each of the seven undulations of the serpent stands a god, who is adjured by Horus to aid in the work of destruction. From the text we learn that the chief offences with which these enemies are charged is the "putting of secret things behind them, the dragging forth of the sacred object *sekem* from the secret place, or sanctuary, and the profanation of certain of the hidden things of the Ṭuat"; because of these things they are doomed to have their bodies first hacked in pieces, and then burned, and their souls utterly annihilated.

CHAPTER XII.

TENTH DIVISION OF THE ṬUAT.

I. KINGDOM OF TEMU-KHEPERÅ-RĀ ACCORDING TO THE BOOK ÅM-ṬUAT.

THE TENTH and ELEVENTH DIVISIONS, or HOURS, are intended to illustrate the passage of ÅFU-RĀ through the region of ÅḲERT, or ÅUḲERT, that is to say, the Kingdom of the Sun-god of ÅNNU, or Heliopolis. The name of the TENTH DIVISION is METCHET-QAT-UTCHEBU, its gate is called ĀA-KHERPU-MES-ÅRU, and the Hour-goddess is ṬENṬENIT-UḤESET-KHAK-ÅB. The pictures and texts which illustrate and describe this region are of peculiar interest, for they refer to the union of KHEPERÅ with RĀ, i.e., the introduction of the germ of new life into the body of the dead Sun-god, whereby ÅFU-RĀ regains his powers as a living god, and becomes ready to emerge into the light of a new day with glory and splendour. It must be understood that the constitution of this DIVISION is quite different from that of any which we have seen hitherto, and that the gods who are in it are peculiar to the region of Åḳert. It is impossible to say where Åḳert began or ended, but as the Ṭuat of the inhabitants of Heliopolis was represented by it, it follows, perhaps, that it was believed to be situated quite near that city. It is pretty certain that it comprised a part of the Eastern Delta, and that it extended along the eastern bank of the Nile some considerable distance to the south of Memphis, in fact, so far as BAKHAU, the Mountain of Sunrise; if this be so, it follows that when the Boat of ÅFU-RĀ entered this DIVISION the god would have to alter his course from east to south. As the Kingdom of Osiris marked the limit of his journey northwards, and the Boat then turned eastwards, so the northern end of ÅḲERT marked the limit of his journey eastwards, and the Boat then turned southwards.

A glance at the Boat of ÅFU-RĀ as it enters this DIVISION shows us that it is neither being towed nor rowed along. Immediately in front of it (vol. i., p. 209) is the serpent THES-ḤRÅU, with ḤERU-KHENTI, in the form of a black hawk, sitting on its back; on one side is a goddess of the North, and on the other a goddess of the South. Next we have the serpent ĀNKH-TA, (vol. i., p. 210), and then a group of twelve gods, four having disks for heads, and carrying arrows, four carrying javelins, and four carrying bows (vol. i., p. 210, 211). The serpent is the "watcher of the Ṭuat in the holy place of Khenti-Åmenti," and the weapons carried by the twelve gods are to enable them to protect ÅFU-RĀ against his enemies in this region. To the right of the path of ÅFU-RĀ are twelve lakes of water, which are intended to represent the celestial watery abyss of NU, from which the Nile on earth was supposed to obtain its supply. At one end of the scene is Horus, who leans on a staff, and addresses the beings who are seen plunging, and swimming, and floating in the various lakes (vol. i., pp. 226, 227), and bids them to come to ḤĀP-UR, and promises them that their members shall not perish, nor their flesh decay. Who the beings in the water are it is impossible exactly to say, but it is clear that they were supposed to have the power to hinder the progress of the Boat of ÅFU-RĀ, for Horus propitiates them with promises of health and strength, as we have seen above. A little beyond the lakes are four goddesses who "shed light upon the road of RĀ in the thick darkness," and in front of them is the mystic sceptre which represents "SET the Watcher," who "waketh up and travelleth with the god."

To the left of the path of ÅFU-RĀ we see first the god P-ĀNKHI, i.e., "he who is endowed with the property of life," and KHEPER-ĀNKH, in the form of a beetle, who is pushing before him an oval of sand, which either contains his germ, or is intended to represent the ball of eggs which the *Scarabaeus sacer* rolls before him, and which he wishes to take t̤hrough the DIVISION into the Eastern Horizon of the sky (vol. i., p. 216). Then we have the two serpents Menenui supporting a disk, and goddesses of the North and South (vol. i., p. 217). To the right of these are the goddesses NETHETH and KENÅT, who spring from the axe SEṬFIT, which supports a disk. These four goddesses gather together souls on earth, and they purify the mighty spirits in the Ṭuat; they only become visible when ÅFU-RĀ appears, and so soon as he has passed them by they vanish. Beyond these is a long procession of deities who assist ÅFU-RĀ in his journey. The first eight, who are goddesses, stand before the Ape-god called ÅF-ERMEN-MAAT-F, who holds the Eye of Horus, and it is their duty to recite the words of power which shall cause splendour to issue from the Eye of Horus each day, and to sing praises to it (vol. i., pp. 219-221). The other deities only come into being when ÅFU-RĀ utters their names; they live in the shades which are in the mouth of the great god, and then their souls travel with him. Their work is to strip the dead of their swathings, and to break in pieces the enemies of Rā, and to order their destruction.

ELEVENTH DIVISION OF THE ṬUAT.

I. KINGDOM OF TEMU-KHEPERÅ-RĀ ACCORDING TO THE BOOK ÅM-ṬUAT.

The name of this DIVISION, or HOUR, or CITY, is RE-EN-QERERT-ÅPT-KHATU, i.e., "Mouth of the Circle which judgeth bodies," the name of its Gate is SEKHEN-ṬUATIU, i.e., "Embracer of the gods of the Ṭuat," and the Hour-goddess is SEBIT-NEBT-UȦA-KHESEFET-SEBȦ-EM-PERT-F, i.e., "Star, lady of the Boat which repulseth Sebȧ at his appearance." This DIVISION of the ȚUAT was very near the Mountain of the Sunrise, from which the newly-born Sun-god would appear soon after day-break, and the knowledge of the gods in it, and of their forms and names, was believed to ensure to its possessor the power to emerge from the Țuat as a spirit equipped for travelling with the Sun-god over the sky. The Boat of ȦFU-RĀ makes its way through this region, and on looking at it (vol. i., p. 233) we see on its prow a disk of light encircled by a serpent; the disk is that of the star PESȚU, and it "guideth this great god into the ways of the darkness which gradually lighteneth, and illumineth those who are on the earth." The Boat is now towed by twelve gods, who employ as a rope the immensely long serpent MEḤEN, the tail of which is supposed to be fastened to the front of the Boat (vol. i., p. 235); so soon as they have towed the god to the end of this DIVISION, and he has set himself in the horizon, they return to their own places. Immediately in front of these gods are two Crowns, the White and the Red (vol. i., p. 237), which rest each on the back of a uraeus; so soon as ȦFU-RĀ comes three human heads look forth, one from each side of the White Crown, and one from the Red Crown, and they disappear when he has passed by. The leaders of this remarkable procession are four forms of the goddess NEITH of Saïs, who spring into life so soon as the sound of the voice of ÅFU-RĀ is heard; these are Neith the Child, Neith of the White Crown, Neith of the Red Crown, and Neith of the phallus. These goddesses "guard the holy gate of the city of Saïs, which is unknown, and can neither be seen nor looked at."

On the right of the path of ÅFU-RĀ we see the two-headed god ÅPER-ḤRÅ-NEB-TCHETTA, with the Crown of the South on one head, and the Crown of the North on the other. Next come the god TEMU, his body, and his soul, the former in the shape of a serpent with two pairs of human legs and a pair of wings, and the latter in that of a man, with a disk on his head, and his hands stretched out to the wings (vol i., p. 242). In front of these are the body and soul of the Star-god SHEṬU; who follows ÅFU-RĀ and casts the living ones to him every day. All the other deities here represented assist the god in his passage, and help him to arrive on the Horizon of the East.

The region to the left of the Boat is one of fire, and representations of it which we have in the BOOK ÅM-ṬUAT and the BOOK OF GATES may well have suggested the beliefs in a fiery hell that have come down through the centuries to our own time. Quite near the Boat stands Horus, holding in the left hand the snake-headed boomerang, with which he performs deeds of magic; in front of him is the serpent SET-ḤEḤ, i.e., the Everlasting Set, his familiar and messenger (vol. i., p. 249). Horus is watching and directing the destruction of the bodies, souls, shadows, and heads of the enemies of RĀ, and of the damned who are in this DIVISION, which is taking place in five pits of fire. A lioness-headed goddess stands by the side of the first pit which contains the enemies of RĀ; the fire with which they are consumed is supplied by the goddess, who vomits it into one corner of the pit.

The next four pits contain the bodies, souls, shades, and heads respectively, of the damned, the fire being supplied by the goddesses in charge. In the pit following are four beings who are immersed, head downwards, in the depths of its fires (vol. i., pp. 249-253). The texts which refer to the pits of fire show that the beings who were unfortunate enough to be cast into them were hacked in pieces by the goddesses who were over them, and then burned in the fierce fire provided by SET-ḤEḤ and the goddesses until they were consumed. The pits of fire were, of course, suggested by the red, fiery clouds which, with lurid splendour, often herald the sunrise in Egypt. As the sun rose, dispersing as he did so the darkness of night, and the mist and haze which appeared to cling to him, it was natural for the primitive peoples of Egypt to declare that his foes were being burned in his pits or lakes of fire. The redder and brighter the fiery glare, the more effective would the burning up of the foes be thought to be, and it is not difficult to conceive the horror which would rise in the minds of superstitious folk when they saw the day open with a dull or cloudy sky, with no evidence in it that the Sun had defeated the powers of darkness, and had suffered no injury during the night.

The presence of the pits of fire in this DIVISION suggests that we have now practically arrived at the end of the Ṭuat, and, according to the views of those who compiled the original description of ÅḲERT, this is indeed the case. We have, in the Boat of ÅFU-RĀ, now passed through the Ṭuat of Khenti-Åmenti, the Ṭuat of Seker, the Ṭuat of Osiris, lord of Mendes and Busiris, and the Ṭuat of TEMU-KHEPERÅ-RĀ, lord of ÅNNU, i.e., the four great Ṭuats which comprised all the great abodes of the dead of all Egypt. Now to enter this group of Ṭuats it was necessary to pass through a forecourt or antechamber, which for purposes of convenience has been called a DIVISION of the Ṭuat, and before ÅFU-RĀ can emerge from the last of the group of Ṭuats into the light of a new day, he must pass through a region which corresponds to the fore-court of the Ṭuats, and serves actually as a forecourt of the world of light. In the forecourt of the Ṭuats the darkness became deeper and deeper the further it was penetrated, but in the forecourt of the world of light the darkness becomes less and less dense as the day is approached. Considered from this point of view, the Four Ṭuats only contain Ten Divisions, or Hours, which corresponded roughly with the Ten GATES of the Kingdom of Osiris, as set forth in many copies of the

Thẹban Recension of the Book of the Dead. Strictly speaking, the addition of a forecourt to the world of light was unnecessary, but as the Theban priests had added one at the beginning of the Four Ṭuats, symmetry demanded that there should be another supplementary region at their end.

If now we treat the Ten Divisions of the Four Ṭuats as Hours, and assume that the Book of ÀFU-RĀ began its journey through them on an average between six and seven o'clock in the evening, it follows that the god reached the abode of Osiris about midnight, together with those souls who travelled with him. The souls who chose to be judged by Osiris, preferring a heaven full of material delights to spiritual happiness, disembarked, and passed into the Judgment Hall, where they received their sentence, and were made joyful or miserable. For the blessed homesteads were provided, and for the wicked slicings and gashings with knives, and pits of fire, wherein their bodies and souls and shadows were destroyed for ever. The evidence indicates that Osiris passed judgment ou souls each day at midnight, and that the righteous were rewarded with good things shortly afterwards; the wicked also were punished with tortures and burnings, probably soon afterwards, or at all events before the Sun rose on the following day. Thus Osiris in the Ṭuat, and Rā in the world of light, would rejoice in freedom from foes until the time arrived for a new "weighing of words" to take place, and, according to one view, the enemies of Osiris, and the foes of Rā, were consumed in fire together, and it was the smoke and fire of their burning which were seen in the heavens at sunrise. We may now consider the vestibule at the end of the Four Ṭuats, and describe the beings who were in it.

CHAPTER XIII.

NINTH DIVISION OF THE ṬUAT.

II. KINGDOM OF TEMU-KHEPERÅ-RĀ ACCORDING TO THE BOOK OF GATES.

THE NINTH, TENTH and ELEVENTH DIVISIONS of the BOOK OF GATES contain series of pictures and texts which are very hard to explain satisfactorily, and the difficulty is further increased by the fact that only one copy of them is known, i.e., that on the sarcophagus of Seti I. It is quite certain that they cannot refer to the Kingdom of Osiris, and we are driven to conclude that they are intended to illustrate and describe the region of AḲERT, which, as has already been said, formed the Ṭuat to which the worshippers of the Sun-god of Heliopolis relegated the spirits of their dead. The FIRST DIVISION of this remarkable region, i.e., the NINTH in the BOOK OF GATES, is entered by the Gate called ĀAT-SHEFSHEFT, which is guarded by the monster serpent ĀB-TA; a company of gods keep watch outside, and the corridor is swept by flames of fire, and a warder in mummied form stands on guard at each end of it.

When ĀFU-Ra has passed through, and the Gate is closed, the gods outside set up a wail, for they must abide in darkness until he re-appears. So soon as the god has entered the DIVISION four gods of the

Ṭuat appear and take hold of the tow-line, but they cannot advance until a path is cleared for them. The obstacles in their way take the forms of the huge serpent ĀPEP, and a great crocodile, the tail of which is in the form of a serpent's head and neck; the name of the latter monster is given both as SESHSESH and SESSI (vol. ii., pp. 242, 244). These have taken up their positions at the end of the DIVISION, in that portion of the Ṭuat which is not very far from the place of sunrise, and a company of beings appear on behalf of ÅFU-RĀ, and proceed to remove the monsters by means of words of power and magical ceremonies.

The company consists of six men, four apes, and four goddesses; in front of these are three men armed with harpoons, and grasping a rope, which passes over the prostrate body and head of the god ÅAI, its end being held fast in his two hands. ÅAI has on his head a small disk, which is set between two objects that resemble the ears of an ass, and these suggest that the figure is intended to represent a form of the Sun-god. The ass is well known as a type of the Sun-god, and "Eater of the Ass" is equally well known as a name for SET or ĀPEP. In an illustration from the Book of the Dead (Chapter XL.; see above, p. 113), the "Eater of the Ass" is seen biting into the back of an ass, which is being delivered by the scribe Nekht in his character of Osiris. That ÅAI is a solar being, and that he opposes ĀPEP on behalf of Rā, is obvious. It seems, however, that he is in need of the help of the men with harpoons, and of their companions behind them, each of whom holds the ends of a pole or rope (of a net), which is bent in the shape of a bow over his or her head. The men are called Ḥeru-meṭu-ḥekaiu, i.e., "those who are over the words (which have) magical power"; the apes are called Saiu, i.e., producers of magical effects by making knots in ropes, over which they whisper incantations; and the women are called Sait, and work the same kind of magic as the apes. The object which each member of these three groups holds with both hands above his, or her, head is probably a net and, as M. Lefébure has pointed out, it is actually so represented in the tomb of Rameses VI. (?). In the Babylonian legend of the fight between Marduk and Tiāmat, the great she-monster of the deep, the god is made to provide himself with a net with which to entangle her feet. In the Book of the Dead (Chapter cliii.B.) we read of the net Ȧnqet, and in the vignette we see three apes working it, and securing the fish which are caught inside it. As Apep was a monster of the deep, to make use of nets in his capture was a wise decision on the part of the friends of Ȧfu-Rā.

The Apes working the net.

Having taken up their positions for attacking Ȧpep the men with the harpoons work the rope which is attached to Ȧai, the goddesses and the apes shake out their rope nets over their heads, and recite their spells, and the men who know the proper words of power shake out their nets and recite the formulae which shall have the effect of throwing ÅPEP and SESSI into the state of stupefaction wherein it will be easy to slay them. The spells and words of power have their proper effect, the monsters are fascinated and slain, and the path of ÅFU-RĀ is clear.

On the right of the Boat of ÅFU-RĀ is the huge serpent KHEPRI, with a head and a pair of human legs at each end of his body; one head faces north (*or*, west), and the other south (*or*, east). Behind each head is a uraeus, and between the uraei stands "HORUS OF THE ṬUAT," wearing the crowns of the South and North (vol. ii., p. 257). A rope passes under KHEPRI, and on one side is hauled by Eight Powers (SEKHEMIU), and on the other by the "Souls of Åment," who are man-headed; by the "Followers of Thoth," who are ibis-headed; by the "Followers of Horus," who are hawk-headed; and by the "Followers of RĀ," who are ram-headed (vol. ii., pp. 255, 256, 258). It will be noted that the two pairs of legs of KHEPRI face in opposite ways, so that in whichever direction he moves one pair must walk backwards; the Eight Powers have overcome the resistance of the sixteen gods, and the face of Horus of the Ṭuat is towards the rising sun.

On the left of the path of ÅFU-RĀ we see a hawk-headed lion called ḤERU-ÅM-UÅA, i.e., "Horus in the Boat," wearing the Crown of the South; on his back stands the two-headed god Horus-Set (vol. ii., p. 247), whose faces typify Day and Night, and Light and Darkness, and the Sun-gods of the South and North. Above the hind-quarters of the lion is the head of the god Ānā (?), wearing the Crown of the South; on the one side we have four gods of the South assisting in the raising of a column surmounted by the Crown of the South, and on the other four gods of the North assisting in the raising of a column surmounted by the Crown of the North. These ceremonies appear to have some connexion with the magical rites which were performed in Egypt in primitive times in the making ready of the crowns for the Sun-god to wear on his rising. Beyond these gods are: 1. The serpent Shemti, with four heads at each end of his body, and his warder Åpu. 2. The serpent Båta, with a head at each end of his body. 3. The serpent Ṭepi, with four human heads and bodies at each end of his body, and his warder Åbeth. These are faced by two gods who are about to attack these serpents with nets, and who assist Horus by reciting words of power for him.

TENTH DIVISION OF THE ṬUAT.

II. Kingdom of Temu-Kheperå-Rā according to the Book of Gates.

In the Tenth Division, or Hour, which Åfu-Rā enters so soon as he has passed through its Gate, which is called Tcheserit, and is guarded by the monster serpent SETHU, it seems that the reconstitution of the Sun-god took place. The god ÅFU-RĀ is towed by gods of the Ṭuat as before, and in this DIVISION all danger appears to have been removed from his path. First stands UNTI, with two stars, and he lights up the upper heaven; next come four deities of flame and fire, who travel with ÅFU-RĀ and give him light. These are followed by three star-gods, who draw towards them a small boat containing a face which is intended for ÅTEN, or the Sun's Disk. The winged serpent SEMI acts as a guide for the god; BESI, the Flame-god, collects fire to put in the new sun; ĀNKHI, the god of Time, in the form of a serpent, with two faces which look in opposite directions, decrees the length of the new Sun's life; the four goddesses cry "Enter in, O Rā! Hail, come, O Rā!" and the MEḤEN serpent surmounted by the god HORUS-SET, with one bow in the dark, and the other in the light, leads the god into the East of heaven (vol. ii., pp. 266, 267).

On the right of the path of ÅFU-RĀ are the twelve ÅKHEMU-SEKU gods, each with his paddle; they are born each day, and after the new Sun-god has entered his boat they join him, and act as his mariners. Beyond these are twelve goddesses who help to tow the Boat of ÅFU-RĀ just before dawn, and then come a god of the Gates of the Ṭuat, the captain of the gods in the Boat, two gods who order the courses of the stars, a star-god in the form of an ape, the Eye of RĀ, which unites itself to the face of Rā, and the guardian of the

Gate of this DIVISION, who does not leave his place. All the other gods travel onwards to the day with ÅFU-RĀ (vol. ii., pp. 273-278).

On the left of the path of ÅFU-RĀ we again see the serpent ĀPEP. To his neck is attached a chain, which is grasped by the hands of the Four SEṬEFIU gods and the Twelve TCHAṬIU gods, and by the colossal hand ÅMEN-KHAT, and passing over five serpents, to each of which it is attached by a small chain, it disappears into the ground at the feet of the god KHENTI-ÅMENTI. Attached to the five small chains are figures of Seb and of the four children of Horus or Osiris, viz., MEST, ḤĀPI, ṬUAMUTEF, and QEBḤSENNUF. Close to the body of ĀPEP, and lying by the chain which is tied to him, is the goddess SERQ. In front ĀPEP is attacked by the ÅNTIU and ḤENĀTIU gods, who are armed with knives and sticks having curled ends. We have seen that in the NINTH DIVISION Āpep was stupefied by the SAIU and other workers of magic, but here it is clear the defeat of this monster is nearly complete. Now that he has been removed from the path of ÅFU-RĀ, and lies fettered, the great god can continue his journey in peace.

ELEVENTH DIVISION OF THE ṬUAT.

II. KINGDOM OF TEMU-KHEPERÅ-RĀ ACCORDING TO THE BOOK OF GATES.

The gate which leads into the ELEVENTH DIVISION, or HOUR, is called SHETAT-BESU, and the name of the monster serpent which guards it is ÅM-NETU-F. Mummied forms guard the corridor between the walls of the outworks, but the place of the company of gods who usually stand outside is occupied by two sceptres, or standards, one of which represents SAR, i.e., Osiris, and the other HORUS. The god ÅFU-RĀ enters this DIVISION in the form in which he has hitherto appeared, and he is towed by four gods who belong to it; we see, however, that ĀPEP has not been wholly removed from the path of the god. The serpent lies here (vol. ii., p. 287) in fetters, and a company of the servants of ÅFU-RĀ who live in this DIVISION stand ready to attack him with the knives which they hold in their hands; their sceptres betoken their position as chiefs in the DIVISION. Next come four apes, each holding a large hand, and these stand, according to the text, two on the right and two on the left of the abode of the god; they hold up the Disk of the god, and sing praises to his soul when it looks upon them. In front of these are the goddesses ÅMENTET and ḤERIT, and the god SEBEKHTI, who presides over the entrance into the vestibule of the world of light.

On the right of the path of the Boat of ÅFU-RĀ are gods and goddesses of the South and North who stablish crowns on the head of Rā when he appears in the sky; gods who give names to Rā and all his forms; gods and goddesses who lament when Rā has gone out from Åment, and who drive away Set; and gods with bowed heads who sing praises to Rā and keep guard over the Hidden Door. The souls of these gods follow after Rā, and accompany him on his way, but their bodies stay always where we see them. Their guardian is (vol. ii., pp. 296-299) the god called MÅTI, who has the head of a cat or lion.

On the left of the path of the Boat of ÅFU-RĀ is a company of his ministers who perform various important duties for him. Four of them carry disks, and give the command to the Gate of ÅḲERT so that the god may be allowed to pass through and set himself in the sky. The mention of ÅḲERT in the text which refers to these is interesting, for it shows that the ELEVENTH DIVISION of the BOOK OF GATES represents a portion of the Kingdom of the Sun-god of Heliopolis. Four other gods carry stars, and when ÅFU-RĀ passes out of this DIVISION, and is received into the arms of NU, the Sky-god, they shout hymns of praise.[1] Before these are twelve gods with sceptres, four ḥaving human heads, four the heads of rams, and four the heads of hawks. The first four are the lords of the region, and stablish the domains of Rā in the sky; the second four provide offerings of bread and water for the god; and the third four set the shrine of Rā in the Mātet-Seḳtet Boat, and place in it the paddles whereby it is to be paddled across the sky. The eight star-goddesses who sit upon uraei belong to the abode of the great god, four coming from the East and four from the West;

[1] Compare Job xxxviii. 7—"When the morning stars sang together, and all the sons of God shouted for joy."

they invoke the Spirits of the East, and join with them in singing hymns to the god, and in praising him after he has appeared in the sky. At the head of the whole company stands a god with the head of a crocodile (vol. ii., pp. 290-293). The Kingdom of TEMU-KHEPERȦ-RĀ differs from other Ṭuats from the fact that, according to the BOOK OF GATES, it contains no place specially set apart for the punishment of the enemies of Osiris and Rā, and of the damned. The pictures which illustrate it supply us with representations of the enemies of the Sun-god and of the beings who vanquish them, and secure his triumphant progress. Having arrived at the end of the ELEVENTH DIVISION the Boat comes to the end of the Fourth Ṭuat;[1] ȦFU-RĀ has effected his transformation as KHEPERȦ, and is now ready to appear in the sky of this world as RĀ. How he effects this we shall see from the next DIVISION.

[1] The Four Ṭuats are the Kingdoms of Khenti-Ȧmenti-Osiris, Seker, Osiris of Mendes and Busiris, and Temu-Kheperȧ-Rā.

CHAPTER XIV.

TWELFTH DIVISION OF THE ṬUAT.

II. EASTERN VESTIBULE OF THE ṬUAT, OR THE ANTE-CHAMBER OF THE WORLD OF LIGHT ACCORDING TO THE BOOK ȦM-ṬUAT.

THE TWELFTH DIVISION, or HOUR, or CITY, is called KHEPER-KEKIU-KHĀU-MESTU, the name of its Gate is THEN-NETERU, and the Hour-goddess is MAA-NEFERT-RĀ; it is the "uttermost limit of thick darkness," i.e., it is not a part of the Ṭuat proper, and it contains the great celestial watery abyss NU, and the goddess NUT. who is here the personification of the " womb of the morning." So soon as the Sun-god passes from the thighs of Nut he will enter the Māṭet Boat, and begin his course in the world of light. We see ȦFU-RĀ in his Boat as before, and in the front of it is the Beetle of Kheperȧ, under whose form the god is to be re-born. The space in front of the Boat is filled by the body of a huge serpent called ĀNKH-NETERU, which lives upon the rumblings of the earth, and from the mouth of which *ȧmakhiu*, or loyal servants, go forth daily. Twelve *ȧmakhiu* of Rā now take hold of the tow-line, and entering in at the tail of the serpent ȦNKH-NETERU draw ȦFU-RĀ and his Boat through its body, and bring him out at its mouth (vol. i., p. 263). During his passage through the serpent, the god transforms himself into Kheperȧ and the twelve *ȧmakhiu* who have been with him throughout his journey in the Ṭuat are, after they have passed out of the serpent's body, re-born on the earth each day. They enter the tail of the serpent as loyal servants, but, like their master, are transformed during their passage through its body, and they emerge from its mouth as "rejuvenated forms of RĀ" ( ) each day. They live on the earth during the day, but at sunset they rejoin their lord, and re-enter the Ṭuat; whilst they are upon earth to utter the name of the god is forbidden to them.

The transformation of the dead Sun-god into the living Kheperȧ having been effected, twelve goddesses step forward when he emerges from the serpent, and tow the great god into the sky, and lead him along the ways of the upper sky. "They bring with them the soft winds and breezes which accompany the dawn, and guide the god to SHU," who is the personification of the atmosphere and of whatever is in the vault of heaven. Of this god are seen (vol. i., p. 277) only the head and arms, and when the Beetle of Kheperȧ comes to him, he receives him, and places the newly-born Sun-god in the opening in the centre of the semi-circular wall which ends this vestibule of the world of light, where he is seen by the people on earth in the form of a disk. This disk either represents a transformation of the Sun-god effected by Shu, or the celestial ball containing the germs of life, of which the type on earth is the ball of eggs which the sacred beetle is seen rolling along the ground. The mummified form in which the dead Sun-god travelled through the Ṭuat is now useless, and we see it cast aside and lying against the wall which divides the Ṭuat from this world; that there shall be no doubt about this it is described by the words "Image (or, form) of ÅF" ().

Turning now to the beings who are on the right and left of the path of the god, we see in the upper register twelve goddesses, each of whom bears on her shoulders a serpent which produces light by belching fire from its mouth (vol. i., pp. 265, 266); these drive away ĀPEP, and frighten the beings of darkness by their fires. Next to these are twelve gods who sing praises at dawn to the god, whom they assert to be "self-begotten" and the author of his own being, and they rejoice because at his new birth his soul will be in heaven, and his body on earth. These gods are indeed spirits of the East, and they are declared to have jurisdiction over the gods of the "land of the turquoise," i.e., Sinai. In the lower register we have a company of twenty-three gods (vol. i., pp. 271-274) who stand in the sky ready to receive Rā when he appears, and to praise him; some of them drive ĀPEP to "the

back of the sky," some support the Great Disk in the sky, and the duty of one of them, who is called SENMEKHEF and appears in the form of a serpent, is to burn up the enemies of Rā at dawn. Thus the Sun-god passed out of the Ṭuat even as he entered it, with praises, and as he did so he bade farewell to Osiris, the Lord of the Ṭuat, under one of whose forms he had completed successfully his journey, in these words:—
"Life to thee! O thou who art over the darkness! "Life [to thee]! in all thy majesty. Life to thee! O "KHENTI-ÀMENTET-OSIRIS, who art over the beings of "Àmentet. Life to thee! Life to thee! O thou who "art over the Ṭuat. The winds of Rā are in thy "nostrils, and the nourishment of Kheperà is with "thee. Thou livest, and ye live. Hail to Osiris, the "lord of the living, that is to say, of the gods who are "with Osiris, and who came into being with him the "first time."

TWELFTH D VISION OF THE ṬUAT.

II. EASTERN VESTIBULE OF THE ṬUAT ACCORDING TO THE BOOK OF GATES.

The last section of the BOOK OF GATES contains representations of the Gate ṬESERT-BAIU, with its two doors (vol. ii., pp. 302, 303), which lead into that portion of the sky wherein the sun rises, and of the stablishing of the Sun-god in his Boat in the sky. This Gate has no company of gods in mummied forms to guard it, and in front of it are two standards, or sceptres, each of which is surrounded by a human head; above that on the left is the Beetle of KHEPERȦ, and over the other is the Disk of TEMU. In other words, the Gate is guarded by symbols of the rising and the setting sun. The corridor between the walls is swept by flames as before, and a warder in mummied form guards each end of it; the one, PAI or BAI, represents the dawn, and the other, ȦKHEKHI, the evening. Within the Gate are two doors, one guarded by the monster serpent SEBI, and the other by the monster serpent RERI. At the threshold is the uraeus of NEPHTHYS, and by the lintel is the uraeus of ISIS, for these goddesses guard this "Secret Gate."

The god ȦFU-RĀ having, as we have seen, transformed himself into KHEPERȦ, and, by the help of the god whose operations have been described, provided himself with a new face, or disk, and new light and fire, passes through the Gate ṬESERT-BAIU, which marks the end of the ṬUAT, into the Vestibule of the world of light. We no longer see him in the form of a ram-headed man, standing under the folds of the serpent MEḤEN, but he appears as KHEPERȦ, i.e., as his Beetle, with the disk in front of him. From the scene which ends the BOOK OF GATES we learn that so soon as the god passes through the Gate of ṬESERT-BAIU he enters the waters of NU, the god of the primeval watery abyss of the sky. The ministers of KHEPERȦ now appear with the MĀṬET-SEḲTET BOAT which they have in readiness, and the god takes his place in it, with the gods who are to guide and propel it. Nu then lifts the Boat up above his head, and the goddess Nut receives the Disk of the sun in her hands. It will be noted that she stands on the head of a god whose body is bent in such a way that it forms a circle: the explanatory text shows that the god is Osiris, and that his body is the Ṭuat. Thus we see that the "womb of Nut," 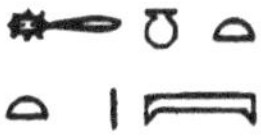, from which the Sun-god is said to be born, lies quite close to the eastern end of the Ṭuat, and that it forms by itself the Vestibule which leads into the world of light.

Close to the high prow of the Boat we see (vol. ii., p. 303) the sun's disk passing through a gap in the mountain which divides the Eastern Vestibule of the Ṭuat from the sky of this world; this disk is the same which we have seen Nut receive from the Beetle of Kheperà, and whilst it is traversing the gap dawn is taking place on the earth. When the disk is on the horizon all men know that the monsters of the Ṭuat have failed to destroy Àfu-Rā or to obstruct his passage, that the god has, with the aid of Kheperà, made all his transformations, that he has appeared in the sky again, full of light, and fire, and life, and that for another day at least all will be well with the world. Meanwhile the souls of the blessed who have travelled through the Ṭuat in the Boat with Àfu-Rā have escaped with him from all its dangers, and have made their transformations as he has done, and now they rise with him above this earth, and are able to look once again upon their own homes and haunts, and friends. Their companions are the gods who minister to Rā, and as they live upon the food of Rā, and are arrayed in his apparel, they become in all respects like him.

For the beings who were left in the Ṭuat, i.e., for those who were not provided for by Osiris in SEKHET-ȦARU and SEKHET-ḤETEPET, existence must have been a sad one, for they were obliged to sit in darkness and misery, except for the brief space each night when ȦFU-RĀ passed through their DIVISIONS, when the gods who were in his train lightened the darkness with the fire which proceeded from their bodies, and the god himself, taking pity on those to whom the making of offerings on earth had ceased, spoke the words which procured sustenance for them. Such acts of grace, however, cannot have been sufficient to secure the happiness of those upon whom they were bestowed, for, with every mention in the texts of the closing of the door of a DIVISION after the god has passed through it, we read that the souls who were outside the door uttered cries of lamentation and wailed bitterly.

It must be remembered that views such as are here described were held only by the priests of ȦMEN-RĀ, who, as we have seen, tried to show that their god was lord of all the Ṭuats of Egypt, and that all the gods of the dead, including even Osiris, and all the blessed, depended upon him for light and food, which they received from him in return for the services which they rendered to him as their overlord. Those who held not these views, and were not followers of Osiris, believed, as did all the primitive Egyptians, that the Ṭuat was a place of darkness, hunger, thirst, and misery, and finally of annihilation. They had no belief either in purgatory or in everlasting punishment; the beings in the Ṭuat lived just so long as their friends and relatives on earth made the prescribed funeral offerings on their behalf, and no longer. The shadows, souls, and bodies of those who were without food in the Ṭuat were, together with the fiends and monsters which opposed the progress of the Sun-god, destroyed by fire each day, utterly and finally; but each day brought its own supply of the enemies of Rā, and of the dead, and the beings which were consumed in the pits of fire one day were not the *same*, though they belonged to the *same classes*, as those which had been burnt up the day before.

INDEX

ÅĀA-KHERU, iii. 31
Āa-Ater, i. 14
Åāḥmes I., iii. 17
Åai, a god, ii. 241, 242; iii. 183, 184
Åaiu, the, ii. 244
Āāiu-f-em-kha-nef, i. 243
Åakeb, iii. 69
Åakebi, Circle, i. 174; iii. 155
Åākhebu, i. 272
Āa-kheperu-mes-åru, i. 208; ii. 34; iii. 99, 172
Āa-kher (?), ii. 171
Āamu, ii. 151, 153, 155; iii. 146
Åānā, i. 29
Åāret-ānkh, i. 183
Āat-åaṭet, i. 197
Āat-åru, i. 200
Åatenkhu, iii. 38
Āat-khu, i. 198
Aats, the Fifteen, iii. 38
Aat-setekau, i. 183, 184; iii. 155
Aat-shefsheft, ii. 237; iii. 101, 182
Aau, i. 14; ii. 139
Āb, i. 31
Ab, i. 15
Abåben, i. 9
Abbott Papyrus, iii. 8
Ābebuiti, ii. 244
Ābenti, i. 8
Ābesh, ii. 262
Åbeth, ii. 248, 251, 252; iii. 186
Ābet-neteru-s, i. 219
Āb-shā-åm-Ṭuat, i. 159; iii. 153
Āb-shāu, i. 160; ii. 27
Åbta, i. 9; ii. 237, 239; iii. 101, 182
Abti, i. 13

Ȧbṭu, iii. 69
Āb-Ṭuat, i. 74
Ābui, i. 109
Abydos, iii. 41, 51, 90, 109, 130, 131, 142, 149
Ȧf, i. 3, 21, 22, 40, 45
Ȧf, Image of, i. 278
Ȧf, a sphinx, i. 94
Ȧf, a fiend, ii. 117, 118; iii. 130
Ȧfa, i. 9
Āfat, ii. 170
Ȧfau, i. 33
Ȧf-ermen-maat-f, i. 220, 221; iii. 175
Ȧffi, i. 176
Af-Rā, i. 116
Ȧfu, i. 120, 140, 188
Ȧfu-Ȧsȧr, i. 148
Ȧfu-ḥer-khent-f, i. 28
Ȧfu-Rā, iii. 106 ff.; as Kheperȧ, i. 257
Ȧfu-Tem, i. 153
Āḥā-ȧb, i. 272
Āḥā-an-urṭ-f, i. 162; ii. 30; iii. 98, 154
Āḥakher, iii. 69
Āḥā-neteru, City, ii. 16; iii. 97, 134
Āḥā-rer, i. 260
Āḥā-Sekhet, i. 206
t, i. 220
Āḥāu, i. 57; ii. 4
Āḥeṭ Chamber, } i. 77, 81
Āḥeth Chamber, }
Āḥi, i. 131
Aimenepthab, ii. 47
Aḳeb, iii. 69
Aḳebsen, i. 56
Ȧkebtit, i. 53
Ȧken-ȧb, i. 9
Ȧken-tauk-ha-kheru, iii. 31
Ȧkenti, iii. 34
Ȧḳert, i. 215; ii. 34, 91, 183, 189, 224, 291; iii. 169, 172, 173, 179, 182
Ȧkesi, iii. 40
Akhabit, i. 32; iii. 113
Ākha-en-Maāt, ii. 190, 192; iii. 101, 166
Ākha-ḥrȧ, ii. 191
Ȧkhekhi, ii. 301; iii. 196
Ȧkhem-ḥemi-f, i. 190
Ȧkhem-ḥep-f, i. 190
Ȧkhem-khemes-f, i. 190
Ȧkhem-sek-f, i. 188
Ȧkhemu-seku, the Twelve, ii. 273, 274, 276; iii. 69, 187
Ȧkhemu-uatchu, iii. 69
Akhem-urṭ-f, i. 188
Ȧḳiu, ii. 222; iii. 169
Ȧkkit-ḥebset-bak-, etc., iii. 34

Alabastronpolis, ii. 45
Al-Barsha, iii. 11, 13, 28, 57, 67
Ale of Maāt, ii. 136
Åma, i. 234
Ām-ā, ii. 162; iii. 160
Ām-āa, ii. 5
Åmakhiu, iii. 192
Āmāma-kheftiu, i. 30
Amamu, Coffin of, iii. 11, 12
Amasis, iii. 17
Ām-āua, ii. 100
Ambenti apes, i. 19
Amem (?), i. 177
Amemet, iii. 51
Åmen of Thebes, i. 166; iii. 16; cult of, iii. 17 ff.
Åmen, a serpent, i. 78; iii. 133
Amen-em-ḥāt III., iii. 15
Amen-em-ḥāt, an officer, iii. 7
Amen-Ḥeru, i. 222
Amen-ḥetep I., iii. 17
Amen-ḥetep II., iii. 81
Amen-ḥetep III., iii. 23, 81
Amen-khat, iii. 188
Amen-khu, i. 222
Amennu-āāiu, etc., ii. 195-197
Amenophath, ii. 47
Amen-Rā, iii. 19-22, 92; cult of, 138
Amen-ren-f, ii. 286
Ament, Åmentet, a goddess, i. 90; iii. 189
Ament, Amentet, i. 1, 15, 267, 276; ii. 21, 85, 149; iii. 97; the beautiful, i. 159; a division of the Ṭuat, i. 85, 89; hidden gate of, ii. 305; hidden path of, i. 123, 146, 151; hidden Circles of, i, 162, 187, 215
Ament, Circle of, ii. 16; iii. 134
Ament, Horn of, i. 1; ii. 1
Ament, Souls of, ii. 253
Amentet, the First Aat, iii. 38
Amentet-ermen, i. 157
Amentet-nefert, i. 30
Ament-semu-set, i. 117
Åment-sethau, ii. 13; iii. 97, 132
Åment-urt, i. 9
Amenti, god, i. 57
Amenti, goddess, i. 101
Åmentit, goddess, ii. 284, 288
Amhetetu Apes, i. 19
Ām-ḥuat-ent-peḥui-f, iii. 31

Àm-kar, i. 13
Ām-kheru, i. 30
Ām-khu, i. 134, 135; iii. 151
Àmkhui, i. 260
Ammāḥet, i. 101; iii. 136, 137
Ammeḥet, ii. 13, 14; iii. 23
Ammeḥet, the Sixth Aat, iii. 39
Ammi-uȧu-f, ii. 288, 291
Ammui, ii. 38
Àm-nebȧui, iii. 96, 114
Am-neter, i. 274
Àm-netu-f, ii. 279, 281; iii. 101, 189
Àm-sekhet-f, i. 203
Àm-ta, i. 48
Àm-ta Boat, i. 42
Àmt-ḥāt-nebt, etc., iii. 35
Àmt-khen-tepeḥ, etc., iii. 36
Àm-Ṭuat, Book of, see Vol. I.; Summary of, ii. 1 ff.; described, iii. 23, 80 ff.; divisions of, iii. 96 ff.; compared with Book of Gates, iii. 103, ff.
Amu, i. 234
Āmu, a god, i. 109
Āmu-āa, i. 31; iii. 115
Amulets, iii. 7
Ānā, ii. 247; iii. 186
Àn-ȧt, i. 109
Ànenruṭ, i. 135
Ànhai, Papyrus of, iii. 59, 63, 64
Ànḥefta, ii. 237
Àn-ḥetep, i. 86
Àn-ḥrȧ, iii. 31
Ani, judgment of, iii. 50-52
Ani, Papyrus of, iii. 37, 44, 47
Ànith, i. 157
Ānkhȧapau, i. 98; iii. 136
Ānkh-ȧb, i. 102
Ānkh-ȧru-tchefau-ānkh-ȧru, i. 148
Ānkh-em-fenṭu, iii. 31
Ānkhet, i. 73, 200
Ānkhet-ermen, i. 262
Ānkhet-kheperu, i. 62; iii. 97, 132
Ānkh-ḥrȧ, i. 131
Ānkhi, ii. 263, 267; iii. 187
Ānkhit, i. 148
Ānkh-kheperu, ii. 13
Ānkh-neteru, i. 259, 261, 264, 265; iii. 192, 193
Ānkhta, i. 209, 210; iii. 173
Ānkhuith, . 147
Ànku, i. 150, 153

Ȧn-maat-Rā-seḥetep-neteru, i. 51
Ȧnnu (Ḥeliopolis), ii. 65; iii. 65, 150, 179; priests of, iii. 4
Ȧnp-heni, i. 102, 103
Ȧnpu, i. 25, 50, 70; ii. 50, 52; iii. 133; standard of, i. 25
Ȧnqet, the net, iii. 183
Ȧntet, i. 51
Ȧnth, i. 51
Ȧntheth, i. 132
Antinoë, iii. 12
Ȧntiu gods, ii. 268, 271; iii. 188
Ȧnt-sekheṭu, i. 251, 253
Anubis, i. 51; ii. 161, 163; iii. 113, 133, 159, 160
Ȧp, Ȧpt (Karnak), iii. 16
Ȧp-ȧst, i. 14
Ape, ii. 161, 163
Ape-god, iii. 175
Apes, the Four, ii. 283, 288; companies of, i. 19; ii. i. 107
Āpep, i. 41, 122, 140, 141-143, 145, 146, 267, 268, 275; ii. 25, 26, 94, 113, 116-118, 241-244, 268, 271, 272, 283, 286; iii. 112, 129, 149, 183-185, 194; chained, iii. 188
Āper-ḥrȧ-neb-tchetta, i. 240, 241; iii. 177
Ȧpert-re, i. 15
Ȧpi-ent-qaḥu, iii. 40
Ȧp-sekhemti, i. 11
Ȧp-she, i. 14, 200
Ȧpt-taui, i. 243
Ȧp-Ṭuat, i. 74
Ȧpu, i. 137; ii. 248-252; iii. 151, 186
Ȧp-uat, i. 4, 11, 22, 25; iii. 105; standard of, i. 25
Āqa-sa, ii. 170
Aqehi, ii. 100, 102, 103; iii. 100, 125
Āqen, ii. 208, 209; iii. 167
Arȧ, i. 14
Ar-ȧst-nefer, i. 31
Ares, ii. 126; iii. 141
Ȧri-āneb-fi, i. 176
Ȧri-en-ȧb-f, iii. 49
Ȧri-tcheru, i. 49
Ȧrit, ii. 139; iii. 100, 143
Ārits, the Seven, iii. 28-31
Ȧrit-ȧru, i. 158
Ȧrit-khu, i. 158
Ȧriti, i. 194
Ārit-Tatheth, i. 219
Ȧr-meḥiu, i. 102
Ȧrnebaui, i. 6, 36; iii. 96
Ȧr-nefertu, i. 66
Arrows, gods with, iii. 173

Arrows of Rā, i. 177
Ārtet, i. 8; iii. 107
Ȧrt-neter-s, i. 15
Ȧsȧr (Osiris), i. 137; iii. 151
Ȧsȧr-ām-ȧb-neteru, i. 124
Ȧsȧr-Ȧsti, i. 56
Ȧsȧr-Bȧtti, i. 57
Ȧsȧr-ḥer-khenṭu-f, i. 57
Ȧsȧr-ka-Ȧmentet, i. 57
Ȧsȧr-khent-Ȧmentet, i. 56
Ȧsȧr-kherp-neteru, i. 57
Ȧsȧr-neb-Ȧmentet, i. 56
Ȧsȧr-Thet-ḥeḥ, i. 56
Ases, iii. 39
Ashebu, iii. 31
Āshemth, ii. 288, 291
Ȧsh-ḥrȧu, i. 120; iii. 149
Ȧs-neteru, i. 173, 174; iii. 155
Asphaltitis Lacus, iii. 128
Ass, the, ii. 242
Ass, Eater of the, ii. 4; iii. 113
Ȧst, i. 15
Ȧst-Amḥit, i. 124
Ȧstcheṭet em-Ȧment, iii. 40
Ȧsth-meḥit, i. 124
Ȧsti-neter, i. 194
Ȧsti-Paut, i. 194
Ȧst-netcht, i. 27
Asyûṭ, Princes of, iii. 7
Ȧtemti, i. 56
Ȧten, ii. 183; iii. 187
Ȧtert, ii. 292
Ȧterti, i. 178, 180-183; ii. 244
Ȧterti, goddesses of, ii. 293
Ātet Boat, i. 7
Ȧth, i. 147
Ȧthep, i. 274
Ȧthpi, i. 236
Ȧṭu, iii. 40
Ȧu (?), i. 260
Āuai, i. 53
Ȧu-ānkhiu-f, i. 260
Āu-āu, i. 69
Āu-em-āāui, i. 243
Ȧuf-ānkh, Papyrus of, iii. 60, 63
Ȧuḳert, ii. 218; iii. 172
Āu-matu, i. 47
Ȧunith, i. 157
Āutu-maāmu-kheru-Maāt, ii. 175
Avaris, iii. 17
Axe, the Seṭfit, i. 218

BA, ii. 88
Baferkheftiu, i. 106
Bai, iii. 196
Baillet, J., iii. 67
Baiu-ȧmmiu-Ṭuat, ii. 16; iii. 134

Baiu-reth-ámmiu-Ṭuat, ii. 142
Baiu-shetaiu, ii. 9; iii. 121
Baiu-Ṭuati, ii. 4, 5; iii. 115
Bák, i. 46
Báket, i. 46
Ba-khati, i. 58
Bakhau, Mount, iii. 150, 173
Balance in Hall of Osiris, ii. 161, 164; iii. 50; guardian of, iii. 50
Bānti, ii. 274, 278
Bark of the Ṭuat, ii. 106
Barley in Ṭuat, iii. 42
Báta, i. 9; ii. 248, 251, 252; iii. 186
Bathers, ii. 223; iii. 169
Bath-resth, i. 102
Baṭi-ṭesheru-, etc., iii. 36
Bátiu, i. 118; iii. 148
Beba, iii. 13
Bebā-áb, ii. 88
Bees, i. 171; iii. 155
Beetle of Kheperá, ii. 301, 303, 305; iii. 135, 149
Beetle Kheper-Ānkh, iii. 174
Beḥā-áb, ii. 88
Beḥent, i. 14
Bekhkhi, ii. 219; iii. 101, 168
Bekhkhit, i, 230
Belzoni, G., ii. 43, 71
Benbenti, i. 8
Benen, ii. 219
Benni, i. 78
Benth, i. 9
Benti, i. 29
Benti-ár-áḥet-f, i. 125
Bes-áru, ii. 32
Besi, i. 13; ii. 263, 266, 267; iii. 187
Besit, i. 14
Best-áru-ānkhet-kheperu, i. 186, 187; iii. 98, 156
Besuā, i. 31
Beq, i. 260
Bet-neter-s, i. 262
Bibân-al Mulûk, ii. 43; iii. 21
Birch, Dr. S., iii. 11
Birds, twittering of, i. 184
Blackden, ii. 243
Black Land, ii. 154
Blessed, the, iii. 142
Boat of Áfu-Rā, iii. 121
Boat of Hathor, i. 24
Boat of Lizard-god, i. 25
Boat of Millions of Years, iii. 20, 24, 95, 138, 166
Boat of Neper, i. 27
Boat of Rā, ii. 277; iii. 21, 72, 104

Boat of the Earth, ii. 106; iii. 115, 126, 127
Boat of the Full Moon, i. 23
Boat of Ṭuat, ii. 107
Boeser, Dr., iii. 84
Boiling Lake, ii. 109; iii. 129
Bonomi, J., ii. 46; iii. 86
Book of Coming Forth by Day, iii. 19, 23, 25, 64, 73
Book of Gates, ii. 43 ff. iii. 23, 24, 25, 85, 100, 103, ff.
Book of Hell, iii. 84, 85
Book of the Dead, ii. 47; Recensions of, iii. 2, 11, 12, 14, 28, 54, 71; Chapters 72 and 89, ii. 59 ff.
Book of Two Ways, iii. 12, 13
Bouriant, U., iii. 82
Bows, gods with, iii. 173
Bows, the two, ii. 263, 267
Bread of Ḥu, ii. 136
Bull, the Double, ii. 106; iii. 156
Bulls, i. 175
Bun-ā, i. 272
Busiris, iii. 147, 158
CACKLER, GREAT, iii. 119
Cataract, First, iii. 7
Cats, i. 179; iii. 155
Chains of Āpep, ii. 283
Champollion, i. 5; ii. 157, 160, 162, 164, 166, 170, 171, 175, 178, 180, 285; iii. 81, 83, 158
Chiefs, Great, iii. 130, 157
Children of Horus, i. 135; ii. 273, 283, 286, 287
Circle of Āment, or Āmentet, ii. 13, 16, 32, 34
Circle of Āment-Sethau, ii. 13
Circle of hidden forms, ii. 181
Circle of hidden gods, i. 161
Circle of Sar, i. 141
Circle of Seker, ii. 16; ii 132
Circle of Unti, ii. 276
Circles, the, iii. 155
Circles of Ṭuat, i. 171; ii. 231
City of Āḥā-neteru, ii. 16
City of Kheper-kekui-khāmestu, ii. 38
City of Metch-qa-uṭebu, ii. 34
City of Re-en-qerert-àpt-khat, ii. 36

Coptos, iii. 7
Cord, ii. 146, 150
Corn in the Ṭuat, ii. 178
Corn-god, iii. 165
Criers, the, ii. 263, 267
Crocodile of Maāti, ii. 61
Crook of Osiris, i. 29, 69; iii. 113
Crown of North (Red), iii. 176, 177
Crown of South (White), iii. 176, 177
Crown of the Uraei, ii. 263, 267

DAMNED, the, iii. 142; burning of, iii. 178
Darkness, beginning of, ii. 1; end of, ii. 38
Delta, ii. 61; iii. 17, 91, 158, 173
Dêr al-Baḥari, iii. 8
Dêr an-Nakhla, iii. 11
de Rougé, E., iii. 83
Devéria, iii. 83, 84
Diodorus Siculus, iii. 128
Disk, the, ii. 95, 183, 287; the Great, i. 175; Face of, ii. 263, 266
Disk of Temu, iii. 196
Divers, the, ii. 223; iii. 169
Double Bull, ii. 106
Dümichen, i. 13

EARTH, Boat of, ii. 106
Earth-god, ii. 107; iii. 127
East, spirits of, ii. 292
Eater of spirits, iii. 151
Eater of the Arm, ii. 163
Eater of the Ass, ii. 4; iii. 113, 115, 183
Egg of the Sun, ii. 96, 189
Elysian Fields, iii. 27, 48
Em-ānkhti, i. 69
Emma-ā, i. 152
Em-nu-ur, i. 131
Emta-ā, i. 155
Enemies of Osiris, i. 150; ii. 231, 232; iii. 170
Eneniu, ii. 96; iii. 119
Ennuerkhata, ii. 106, 119; iii. 127
Ennutchi, ii. 140, 144; iii. 144
Eratosthenes, ii. 47
Ermen-ta, ii. 238
Ermenu, i. 236, 272
Ermenui, i. 221
Erṭā, i. 234
Erṭāt-sebanqa, iii. 32
Erṭāu, i. 211
Eye of Horus, i. 221; ii.

65, 67; **iii.** 134, 175; = Sekri, **iii.** 133
Eye of Khuti, **ii.** 265
Eye of Rā, **i.** 51; **ii.** 278

FA (?), **i.** 236
Fa-ȧr-tru, **i.** 33
Face of Rā, **ii.** 266
Face of the Disk, **ii.** 263, 266
Faiu-neteru, **ii.** 266; **iii.** 125
Fa-pet, **iii.** 39
Fashioner, the Great, **ii.** 65
Feather of Maāt, **ii.** 175, 184
Field, Great, **iii.** 69, 70
Field of Metchet-nebt-Ṭuatiu, **ii.** 21
Field of Net-neb, etc., **ii.** 9
Field of Offerings, **iii.** 145
Field of Peace, **i.** 63; **ii.** 150; **iii.** 42, 145
Field of the Khu, **ii.** 149, 150
Field of the Peru, **ii.** 8
Field of Urnes, **i.** 20; **ii.** 4
Fields of the Ṭuat, **ii.** 189
Fire, pits of, **i.** 251; **iii.** 143
Flame-goddess, **ii.** 132
Flesh of Osiris, **iii.** 153
Flesh of Sekri, **i.** 97
Floaters, **i.** 224; **ii.** 223; **iii.** 169
Followers of Horus, **ii.** 253; **iii.** 185
Followers of Kheperȧ, **iii.** 152
Followers of Osiris, **iii.** 153
Followers of Rā, **ii.** 253; **iii.** 153, 185
Followers of Tem, **iii.** 152
Followers of Thoth, **ii.** 253; **iii.** 185
Foster-parents, **iii.** 67
Fraser, W. **ii.** 43

GAP, THE, **iii.** 41, 91, 109
Gate of Āb-ta, **ii.** 237
Gate of Ām-netu-f, **ii.** 279
Gate of Sethu, **ii.** 259-261
Gate of Ṭuati, **ii.** 287
Gates, The Ten, **iii.** 37
Gîza, Pyramids of, **iii.** 94
Gods asleep in Osiris, **ii.** 210; behind the shrine, **ii.** 133, 137; the birth-place of, **iii.** 43; before shrine, **ii.** 135, 137; of doubles, the Twelve; **iii.** 141; of entrances, **ii.** 88; of Boiling Lake, **ii.** 109, 112; of temples, **ii.** 198, 199; the holy, **ii.** 108;

within Ṭuat, ii. 104; of *Kau*, ii. 127
Goodwin, ii. 162, 163, 165; iii. 86
Grain-god, iii. 111, 165
Green-face, i. 69
Guides to Other World, iii. 27

Ḥaāt-em-sepu-s, i. 266
Hahaiu, ii. 160
Ha-ḥetep, iii. 39
Ḥait, i. 53
Hall, H. R., iii. 8, 9
Hall of gods, i. 40
Hall of Judgment, iii, 158
Hall of Osiris, i. 139
Hall of Rā, ii. 96; iii. 163
Ḥām, i. 268
Hand, the Hidden, ii. 272, 273
Ḥāp (Nile), i. 55; iii. 41, 69
Ḥāpi, i. 135; ii. 51, 273; iii. 188
Ḥap-semus, i. 180, 181; iii. 155
Ḥāp-ur, i. 229; iii. 174
Haroeris, ii. 132
Harpoons, ii. 241, 242; iii. 182
Ha-sert, iii. 39
Ḥast, Lake of, iii. 49
Ḥāt-em-taui-s, i. 266
Ḥaṭet-ḥanṭu-s, i. 250
Ḥatet-ketits, i. 249
Hathor, Boat of, i. 24
Hathor-Isis, i. 24; iii. 9
Ḥaṭ-nekenit, i. 250
Ḥaṭ-Nemmȧt-set, i. 251
Ḥaṭ-sefu-s, i. 251
Ḥau serpent, i. 40; iii. 112
Hawk, Black, iii. 173
Hawk, Divine, i. 183
Heart, weighing of, iii. 50
Ḥebs, i. 194,
Ḥebset, i. 180
Hebṭ-re-f, iii. 41
Hefau, ii. 205; iii. 167
Ḥeḥ, ii. 38
Ḥeḥu, i. 271
Ḥeḥut, i. 271; ii. 38
Ḥek, ii. 305
Ḥeka, ii. 89, 91, 122, 140, 191, 222, 240, 262, 282; iii. 109
Ḥekau, ii. 87, 103; iii. 13, 116, 140
Ḥeka-ser, i. 140
Ḥeken-em-ben-f, i. 13
Ḥekennu-Rā, i. 14
Ḥekennutheth, i. 157
Ḥekenu, i. 269
Ḥekent, i. 15, 78, 81; iii. 133

Ḥekent-em-sa-s, i. 10
Heliopolis, ii. 65; iii. 4, 41, 65, 90, 150, 167, 168, 169, 172, 173, 182
Hell, iii. 88
Hem, i. 131
Hembem, i. 14
Ḥemt, i. 132
Ḥenātiu gods, ii. 268, 271; iii. 188
Ḥenbet, i. 20
Ḥenbethem, i. 125
Ḥenbiu gods, the Four, ii. 150; iii. 145, 146
Ḥenḥenith, i. 132
Heniu gods, ii. 146, 148; iii. 145
Ḥen-kherth, i. 78
Ḥenksu, ii. 4
Ḥennu, i. 54
Ḥennu Boat, ii. 51
Ḥenti, i. 131
Ḥenti requ, iii. 33
Ḥent-nut-s, i. 197
Ḥepā, i. 244
Ḥepti-ta-f, i. 190
Ḥept-menȧ-f-ṭuȧ-uȧa-f, i. 27
Ḥepti, ii. 219
Ḥeq-nek-mu, i. 260
Ḥeq-neteru-f, i. 203
Ḥeqes, ii. 190
Ḥer-ȧb-uȧa-set, i. 11
Ḥerakleopolis, iii. 5, 7, 90
Ḥereret serpent, ii. 122, 123, 127; iii. 140
Ḥer-ḥequi, i. 86
Ḥeri-qenbet-f, ii. 142, 146; iii. 144
Ḥerit, ii. 284, 288; iii. 189
Ḥer-khu, i. 86
Ḥer-nest-f, ii. 275, 278
Herpiu, ii. 222; iii. 169
Ḥer-shā-f, i. 50
Ḥer-shāu-s, i. 252
Ḥer-sheta-taui, i. 222
Ḥer-ṭebat, i. 69
Ḥer-ṭesu-f, i. 142; iii. 152
Ḥert-erment, i. 209
Ḥert-ḥatu-s, i. 255
Ḥert-kettut-s, i. 255
Ḥert-nemmȧt-s, i. 255
Ḥert-Ṭuati, i. 30
Ḥeru (Horus), i. 137, 260; ii. 88; iii. 151; standard of, ii. 171
Ḥeru-ȧm-uȧa, iii. 185
Ḥer-uarfu, i. 66
Ḥeru-Ḥekennu, iii. 106
Ḥeru-ḥeken, i. 141
Ḥeru-ḥen, i. 32
Ḥeru-ḥer-khenṭ-f, i. 154
Ḥeru-ḥer-she-ṭuati, i. 203; iii. 157

Ḥeru-khenti, i. 209; iii. 173
Ḥeru-khenti-àḥet-f, i. 125
Ḥeru-kheti, i. 53
Ḥeru-meṭu-ḥekaiu, iii. 184
Ḥeru-shefshefit, i. 98
Ḥeru-Ṭuati, i. 29, 158, 255; ii. 257
Ḥeru-ur, i. 29; ii. 132; iii. 142
Ḥer-utu-f, i. 252, 255
Ḥes-ā, i. 11
Ḥeseq-khefti-set, i. 14
Ḥet-Benben, ii. 196, 200; iii. 167, 168
Ḥetch-ā, i. 11, 31
Ḥetchefu, i. 129
Ḥetchetchtu, i. 32
Ḥetch-nāu, i. 77; iii. 133
Ḥetem-àb, i. 14
Ḥetemet-baiu, iii. 40
Ḥetemet-khemiu, i. 179, 180; iii. 155
Ḥetemet-khu, i. 194
Ḥetemit, i. 230
Ḥetemtit, i. 143
Ḥetep, a god, i. 69; iii. 47-52
Ḥetep-em-khut-s, i. 262
Ḥetepet-neb-s, i. 177-179; iii. 155
Ḥetepet-neter, i. 192
Ḥetepi, the god, ii. 146; iii. 144, 145
Ḥetepit, i. 14
Ḥetep-khenti-Ṭuat, i. 124
Ḥetep-neteru, the eight, i. 109; iii. 137
Ḥetep-neteru-Ṭuat, i. 194; iii. 156
Ḥetep-ta, i. 166
Ḥetepti-kheperu, ii. 175, 178
Ḥeteptiu gods, i. 118, 121, 122, 126; ii. 92, 184; iii. 117, 148, 164
Ḥetep-uàa, i. 190
Ḥetepui, i. 137; iii. 151
Ḥethti, i. 13
Ḥetit, i. 262
Ḥet-nub, ii. 43
Ḥet-stau-kher-āḥa-Rā, i. 130
Ḥet-ṭemṭet-Rā, i. 130
Ḥet-ṭuau-Rā, i. 129
Ḥet-ur-kau, iii. 69
Ḥi, i. 268
Ḥiāt, i. 155
Hidden Flesh, i. 138
Hidden Hand, ii. 272, 273
Hidden mountains, ii. 85
Ḥi-khu- . . . . i. 155
Hippopotamus, iii. 42
Holders of the cord, ii. 146
Holders of time, ii. 151
Honey bees, iii. 155

Horn of Ament, i. 1; ii. 1
Horn of the Sky, i. 259
Horus, i. 69, 173, 278; ii. 135, 136, 151, 253, 255, 262, 288, 291; iii. 50
Horus and Utchat, i. 83
Horus in the Boat, ii. 247
Horus of the Ṭuat, i. 29, 156; ii. 254; iii. 185
Horus the Aged, ii. 132, 231, 232, 234
Horus, the four Children of, i. 135; ii. 47, 273, 283, 286, 287; iii. 151, 188
Horus-Rā, ii. 252
Horus-Set, i. 32; ii. 247, 251, 263, 267; iii. 113, 186, 187
Hours, gods and goddesses of, i. 156, 159; ii. 126, 127, 273, 276, 277, 289; iii. 94, 110, 140, 141, 153
House of Life, ii. 186
House of Osiris, iii. 64, 132, 149
Ḥrȧ-f-ā-f, i. 32
Ḥrȧ-seni, i. 15
Ḥu, i. 4, 141; ii. 136, 305
Ḥuit, i. 10
Ḥu-kheru, iii. 28
Ḥun, i. 32
Ḥunnu, i. 268
Ḥun-sāḥu, i. 53
Ḥunt, i. 10
Ḥuntheth, i. 219
Hyksos, iii. 16, 17

Image of Ȧf, i. 278; ii. 194
Image of Ȧffi, i. 176
Image of Ȧri-āneb-fi, i. 176
Image of Ba-neteru, i. 175
Image of Horus, i. 173
Image of Isis, i. 173
Image of Ka-Ȧmentet, i. 175
Image of Khatri, i. 176
Image of Kheperȧ, i. 144, 171
Image of Nut, i. 172
Image of Osiris, i. 144, 173, 276
Image of Rā, i. 144, 171
Image of Rem-neteru, i. 175
Image of Seb, i. 172
Image of Seker, or Sekri, i. 97; ii. 17; iii. 135
Image of Shu, i. 171, 278
Image of Tefnet, i. 172
Image of Tem, i. 144, 171
Images of Ta-thenen, the Four, i. 168
Isis, i. 22, 140, 141, 173; ii. 26, 50, 305; iii. 134, 155, 196

Isis of Åmentet, i. 85
Isis of the North, i. 124
Isis-Thaȧth, i. 129
Isis, words of, ii. 25
Islands of the Blessed, iii. 58
Iuḥerȧptesu, i. 106

JACKAL-GODS, i. 26; of Lake of Life, ii. 127
Jackal sceptre, ii. 84
Javelins, gods with, iii. 173
Jehannum, iii. 88
Jéquier, iii. 83, 84
Judgment, the, iii. 25, 85; at midnight, iii. 180
Judgment Hall, ii. 158, 159; iii. 158
Judgment Scene, iii. 50

KA-AMENTET, i. 175
Ka-Amenti, ii. 274, 278
Ka-Åru, i. 53
Ka-em-ānkh-neteru, i. 261
Kāf, Jebel, iii. 88
Kahemhemet, i. 129
Ḳai, i. 135
Ka-neteru, i. 14
Kapet, iii. 40
Karnak, iii. 16
Ka-Shu, i. 4, 141; iii. 106
Ka-Ṭuat, i. 14
Ḳebḳa, iii. 14
Ḳeb-ur, i. 278
Kefi, ii. 259
Kekhert (?), i. 154
Keku, i. 182
Kenȧt, i. 218; iii. 175
Ḳenḳenur, iii. 119
Ketuit-ṭent-ba, i. 28
Khā-ā, i. 211
Khā-ba-āa, i. 40
Kharga, iii. 129
Khast-ta-ruṭ, ii. 213
Khatri, i. 176
Khebs-ta, i. 182
Khebt-ḥer-senf-, etc., iii. 36
Kheftes-ḥȧu-, etc., i. 140; iii. 151
Khemit, ii. 17; iii. 139
Khen, i. 48
Khen-en-urṭ-f, i. 47
Khenfu cakes, ii. 188
Khennu, i. 48, 188
Khennu-ermen, i. 272
Khent-Amenti, Khenti-Amenti, i. 4, 165, 213; ii. 117, 118, 132, 135, 136, 137, 230, 273; iii. 91, 108, 109, 130, 131; gods of, iii. 140
Khent-ȧst-f, i. 222
Khenti-Amentet-Osiris, iii. 195

Khent-Ḥeru, i. 209
Khenti-Aukert, iii. 168
Khent-she-f, i. 13
Khenti-theth-f, i. 272
Khenti Ṭuat, ii. 218
Khent-ment-f, i. 222
Khent-unnut-f, i. 190
Khepȧ, i. 258, 259
Khepau, ii. 223 ; iii. 169
Kheper, Kheperȧ, i. 19, 40, 41, 81, 82, 86, 89, 122, 136, 138, 257, 278 ; ii. 34, 36, 301 ; iii. 133, 151, 172 ; unites himself to Rā, i. 215 ; born as Rā, ii. 38
Kheperȧ, Beetle of, iii. 193, 196, 197
Kheperȧ, Image of, i. 144, 171
Kheper-ānkh, i. 215 ; iii. 174
Kheper-en-Asȧr, iii. 107
Kheper-kekiu-khāu-mestu, i. 257 ; ii. 38 ; iii. 99, 192
Khepri serpent, ii. 254, 256, 257, 258 ; iii. 185
Kher-āḥa, iii. 41
Kheru-āḥāu-Ament, the Twelve, iii. 146
Kher-ḥeb, ii. 63
Kherp, the steersman, i. 4
Kheru-āḥāu, ii. 155
Kheru-āmu-pereru, ii. 202
Kheru-ennuḥu-em-Ṭuat, iii. 145
Kheru-Ennutchi, iii. 144
Kheru-khu, the, ii. 287, 290
Kheru-metauḥ, ii. 200-202 ; iii. 167
Kheru-sebau, ii. 287, 290
Kheru-utchat, i. 261
Kheru-ṭep, i. 262
Khesefet-smatet, i. 11
Khesef-ḥrȧ-, etc., ii. 27
Khesfet-hau-, etc., iii. 98
Khesef-ḥrȧ-āsht-kheru, iii. 31
Khesef-ḥrȧ-khemiu, iii. 98
Khesefu, i. 211
Khet-ānkh-f, i. 266
Kheti, serpent, ii. 232, 234, 235 ; iii. 170
Khet-[kheper], i. 162
Khetrȧ, i. 58, 60 ; iii. 97, 122
Khet-uat-en-Rā, i. 265
Khnem-renit, i. 243
Khnemiu, the, ii. 293, 297
Khnemu, i. 55 ; ii. 80, 88, 288, 291
Khnemu-Qenbeti, i. 28
Khnemut, ii. 294

Khu, i.e., the blessed dead, i. 120; ii. 91, 149, 150 ff., 225; iii. 148
Khuai, i. 11
Khu-ȧst, iii. 8
Khui, i. 32
Khu-re, i. 292
Khu-tchet-f, iii. 34
Khuti, i. 138; ii. 87, 95, 96, 103, 116, 117, 120, 130, 140, 150, 169, 191, 200, 220, 271, 272, 280, 304
Khuti, Eyes of, ii. 265
Khut-mu, i. 14
Khut-Ṭuat, i. 200
Kings, Tombs of, ii. 43
Knots, magic worked by, ii. 241
Ḳua-ṭep, ii. 54, 57

Lacau, P., iii. 14, 66
Lady of the Boat, i. 4
Lake of blazing heads, i. 101
Lake of Boiling Water, ii. 109; iii. 128, 129, 136
Lake of Ḥetep, iii. 47
Lake of Life, ii. 127, 131; iii. 141
Lake of Living Uraei, iii. 141
Lake of Serser, ii. 227-230
Lake of Souls, ii. 229
Lake of Uraei, ii. 127, 131
Lakes, the Twelve, i. 224; iii. 174
Land of Seker, ii. 13, 16
Land of Sekṛi, i. 93
Lanzone quoted, i. 225, 256; iii. 83, 89
Lefébure, E., i. 5, 61; ii. 111, 161, 162, 163, 165, 166, 191; iii. 81, 82, 86, 166
Legrain, G., iii. 17
Lepsius, R., iii. 81
Libyans, ii. 151, 153; iii. 146
Life, House of, ii. 127, 131, 186
Life, Lake of, iii. 141
Lion-god, the Double, ii. 63
Living Uraei, ii. 127, 131, 132
Lizard-god, i. 25
Loret, V., iii. 82
Luxor, iii. 16
Lynx-god, i. 150

Maā, i. 244
Maa-ā, i. 11
Maā-ȧb, ii. 158
Maā-ȧb-khenti-ȧḥet-f, i. 125

Maa-en-Rā, i. 9
Maa-nefert-Rā, i. 257; iii. 109, 192
Maa-neter-s, i. 15
Maāt, i. 22, 82, 101, 153; ii. 156, 265, 298; iii. 159
Maāt, ale of, ii. 136
Maāt food, iii. 164
Maāt, ways of, ii. 16
Maa-tcheru, i. 49
Maa-thetef, iii. 40
Maāti, in the Ṭuat, iii. 96
Maāti, Field of, i. 6
Maāti, gods and goddesses of, i. 4; ii. 92, 145, 184, 186; iii. 163, 166
Maāti, Pool of, ii. 61
Maātiu, iii. 117, 118
Maāt-kheru, iii. 130
Māfket, i. 270
Magical names and formulae, iii. 49
Māket-àri-s, i. 11
Makhi, i. 33
Māk-neb-s, ii. 32
Māmu serpent, ii. 201, 202
Mānenui, ii. 47
Mankind, Four Races of, iii. 146
Mānṭit Boat, i. 214
Manu, iii. 104
Marduk, iii. 183
Maspero, Prof., i. 60, 69, 81, 93, 200, 209; iii. 3, 14, 82, 84, 88, 134
Masters of earths, ii. 133
Masters of pits, ii. 133, 137
Masturbation of Rā, ii. 154
Ma-ṭepu-neteru, i. 269
Māṭes-en-neḥeḥ, iii. 132
Māṭes-mau-āt, iii. 132
Māṭes-sma-ta, i. 62; iii. 132
Māṭet Boat, i. 7; ii. 38, 306; iii. 94
Mātet-Sekṭet Boat, iii. 190, 196
Māthenu, i. 167
Mathi, i. 53
Màti, cat-god, ii. 294, 299; iii. 190
Mat-neferu-neb-set, i. 11
Mediterranean Sea, iii. 48
Meḥen, i. 140, 148, 149, 162, 163, 188, 191, 233, 234; ii. 30, 87, 95, 122, 140, 149, 191, 267; iii. 116, 152, 153, 156, 187, 196
Meḥen, used as a tow rope, iii. 176
Meḥen-ta, i. 177, 237
Meḥ-Maāt, i. 54
Meḥni, i. 234

Meḥ-urt, Seven addresses of, iii. 14
Memphis, iii. 4, 5, 10, 11, 90, 131, 147
Men-ā, i. 196
Menȧt, i. 118
Mendes, iii. 65, 91, 147, 158
Meṇenui, i. 216 ; iii. 174
Menḥi, i. 182
Meni, i. 49, 136
Menkert, i. 219
Menkhet, i. 194
Men-Maāt-Rā, ii. 50-69
Menmenut, i. 81 ; iii. 133
Mennu, i. 167
Menthu-ḥetep kings, iii. 7
Menthu-ḥetep II., iii. 7
Menthu-ḥetep III., iii. 8-10
Mer-en-āāiu-f, i. 243
Mer-ent-neteru, i. 248
Mer-setau-āb, etc., iii. 36
Mert-neser, i. 14
Mesekhti, i. 244
Meskh-set, i. 57
Mes-peḥ, iii. 32
Mesperit, i. 12 ; ii. 21 ; iii. 98, 148
Mes-Ptaḥ, iii. 32
Mesqet Chamber, ii. 61
Mest, Mesthȧ, i. 135 : ii. 50, 273 ; iii. 188
Mest-s-tcheses, i. 30
Meṭ, ii. 170
Metchet-[mu]-nebt-Ṭuat, ii. 21 ; iii. 97, 148
Metch-qa-uṭebu, ii. 34
Metchet-qaṭ-utchebu, iii. 172
Meṭ-en-Ȧsȧr, i. 30
Meterui, ii. 155 ; iii. 147
Meṭes, ii. 279
Meṭes-en-neḥeḥ, i. 65
Meṭes-ḥrȧ-ȧri-she, iii. 31
Meṭes-mau-āt, i. 65
Meṭes-sen, iii. 31
Meṭet-qa-utchebu, i. 207, 208 ; iii. 99
Meṭ-ḥrȧ, i. 132
Meṭi, i. 8
Metrui, i. 167
Monkey with star, ii. 274, 278
Morning Star, iii. 135
Mountain of Set, ii. 84 ; the Hidden, ii. 85
Mummy bandages, i. 69
Mu-sta (?), ii. 130
Muthenith, i. 78
Muti-khenti-Ṭuat, i. 191, 192

Nā, i. 264
Nȧb-ḥrȧ, i. 46

Nābti, i. 7
Nȧkith, i. 143
Nāq, ii. 210; iii. 167, 168
Nareḥ, i. 33
Nast-taui-si, etc., iii. 36
Nations, the Four, iii. 146
Nāu, iii. 40
Naville, Prof., iii. 8, 9, 82
Neb-ȧa, i. 268
Neb-Aatti, i. 203
Neba-khu, i. 272
Neb-ȧmakh, i. 260
Neb-ānkh, i. 268
Neb-āqet, i. 222
Nebaui, i. 31
Neb-āut-ȧb, ii. 188; iii. 165
Neb-er-tcher, i. 166
Nebi, iii. 32
Neb-khert-ta, i. 154
Neb-net, i. 49
Neb-Pāt, i. 196
Neb-Rekhit, i. 178
Nebseni, iii. 43, 47, 53, 58, 64, 159
Nebt-ābui, i. 249
Nebt-āḥā, ii. 158: iii. 101, 158
Nebt-āḥāu, ii. 144; iii. 144
Nebt-ānkh, i. 10, 70
Nebt-ānkhiu, i. 248
Nebt-ār-em-uȧa-ȧbt, i. 266
Nebt-ta-ṭesher, i. 11
Nebt-āu-khenti-Ṭuat, i. 192, 193
Neb-tchetta, i. 162
Nebt-en- . . . . . ., i. 157
Nebt-ḥet, i. 15
Nebt-ḥetepu, ii. 217
Nebti, i. 194
Nebtȧm, i. 262
Nebt-khart-āat, iii. 32
Nebt-khu, i. 248
Nebt-mȧt, i. 197
Nebt-meket, i. 9
Nebt-mu-Ṭuatiu, ii. 20
Nebt-nebt, i. 157
Nebt-pet-ḥent, etc., iii. 32
Nebt-Rekeḥ, i. 200
Nebt-rekḥu-resht, iii. 33
Nebt-semu-nifu, i. 175-177; iii. 155
Nebt-senket-āat-, etc., iii. 34
Nebt-seṭau, i. 197
Nebt-seṭau-qat, iii. 31
Nebt-sesesh-ta, i. 265
Nebt-s-tchefau, ii. 119; iii. 100
Nebt-shāt, i. 197
Nebt-shefsheft, i. 197
Nebt-ta-tcheser, i. 32
Nebt-taui, a lake, iii. 48

Nebt-tchefau, iii. 140
Nebt-ṭenṭen-, etc., iii. 36
Nebt-Ṭuat, i. 268
Nebt-uauau, i. 200
Nebt-usha, i. 162; ii. 30; iii. 98, 154
Nebt-uast, i. 48, 147
Nebu-Khert, the Nine, ii. 114; iii. 130
Nectanebus, i. 37
Nefert-ḥek-ṭept, i. 265
Nefert-khā, i. 14
Nefert-khāu, i. 265
Negroes, ii. 151, 153, 155
Neḥa, i. 33
Neḥa-ḥrȧ, i. 26, 27, 40, 56, 141, 143, 214; ii. 272; iii. 112, 152
Neha-kheru, i. 50
Neha-ta, i. 194
Neḥebeti, i. 203
Neheb-kau, i. 74; iii. 40
Nehem-kheru, i. 50
Nehenuit goddesses, i. 20
Nehep, ii. 210-212, 217; iii. 167, 168
Nehes, i. 4, 141
Neḥesu, ii. 151, 153, 155; iii. 146
Nehui, i. 271
Neith, of Saïs, i. 70, 78; of North and South, iii. 107; the Four Forms of, i. 238, 239; iii. 176, 177
Neḳau, iii. 32
Nekent-f, i. 4
Nekhebet, i. 77
Nekht, Papyrus of, iii. 163
Nekht-neb-f, iii. 83
Nemi, ii. 259
Nemt-ṭesu-ubṭet-sebȧu, etc., iii. 35
Nemu, the, ii. 244
Nenḥa, ii. 88
Nepemeḥ, ii. 88
Nepen, i. 7, 31
Neper, corn-god, i. 24, 27, 31; ii. 180
Nepertiu gods, i. 42
Nephthys, i. 22; ii. 305; iii. 195
Neprȧ, ii. 180, 188; iii. 164, 165
Nerta, i. 55, 243
Nerutet-nebt-, etc., iii. 36
Nesert, i. 14; ii. 137; iii. 142
Nesert-ānkhet, i. 184
Neshmekhef, i. 271
Nesti-khenti-Ṭuat, i. 191, 192
Net (Neith), i. 7, 8, 15
Net, the, iii. 184
Nets, gods with, iii. 185

Net-Asȧr, ii. 9; iii. 122
Netch-ȧtef, i. 131
Netchem-ȧb, i. 268
Netchti, i. 132
Neteḳa-ḥrȧ-khesef-aṭu, iii. 31
Neterit, iii. 118
Neter-kher, iii. 70
Neter-khert, ii. 9, 17; iii. 14, 65
Neter-neferu, i. 54
Neter-neteru, i. 190
Netert-en-khentet-Rā, i. 198
Neterti, Khu of, ii. 150
Neṭeru, i. 236
Neteru-ȧmiu, iii. 126
Neteru-ḥeti, ii. 196
Netheth, i. 218; iii. 175
Net-mu, i. 74
Net-neb-uā-kheper-āut, i. 50, 61; ii. 9; iii. 97, 121
Net poles, ii. 244
Net-Rā, i. 6, 20, 40; ii. 1; iii. 3 ff., 96, 105, 108
Net-ṭept-ȧnt, i. 30
Netu, i. 101; iii. 136
Ni, i. 271
Nile, i. 55; ii. 43, 154; iii. 124, 173, 174
North, gods of, ii. 147, 253
Nu, battle-field of, i. 181
Nu, god of celestial abyss, i. 55, 105, 185, 228, 229, 257, 258, 296; ii. 38, 225, 226, 285, 286, 291, 303; iii. 192
Nu, Lake of, iii. 169
Nu of the Ṭuat, i. 85
Nu, Papyrus of, iii. 28, 38
Nubia, iii. 146
Nubians, iii. 17
Nubiu, ii. 222; iii. 169
Nut, i. 172; ii. 38, 47, 53, 54, 57, 59, 65, 67, 69, 244, 256-258, 265, 266, 271, 276, 291, 298, 306; iii. 67, 89, 192; Rā appears in, ii. 303, 304
Nut, a god (?), i. 179
Nut-ent-qaḥu, iii. 40
Nutet, i. 15
Nut-urt, iii. 48

Oimenepthah, ii. 46, 47
Orion, iii. 14, 113
Osiris, i. 149, 173,; ii. 280; iii. 19, 91-93, 194; Birth-place of, i. 7; Eye of Rā, i. 159; Flesh of, iii. 153; Forms of, iii. 56, 57, 148; Four Coffers of, i. 145; House of, iii. 31; Image of, i. 144,

276; Judgment Hall of, ii. 158; seated in judgment, iii. 51, 159, 160
Osiris-khenti-Åmenti, i. 19; iii. 111, 116 ff., 121 ff.
Osiris, secret place of, ii. 25, 26
Osiris = the Ṭuat, ii. 306; iii. 179
Osiris Unnefer, i. 32; iii. 113
Other Worlds, conceptions of, iii. 27 ff.; Guides to, iii. 1 ff.; Valley of, ii. 47

Paddles, ii. 276; iii. 156
Pai, ii. 301; iii. 196
Pakhet, i. 48
Pȧn, i. 31
Pān-ȧri, i. 206
P-ānkhi, i. 215; iii. 174
Patheth, i. 13
Pa-ur, iii. 69
Pe, city of, ii. 61
Peace, Lake of, iii. 47
Pebaf, i. 53
Peḥiu, ii. 65
Penṭer, ii. 288, 291
Pepi I., iii. 3
Pepi II., iii. 1
Per-em-hru, iii. 28, 64, 65, 66
Peremu (?), i. 167
Perit, i. 197
Periu, ii. 288, 290
Pert-em-ȧp, i. 266
Pertiu gods, iii. 112, 122
Peru gods, ii. 8
Pesi, i. 252
Pesṭ, i. 233
Pesṭet, i. 234
Pesṭit, ii. 190; iii. 101, 166
Pesṭu star, iii. 176
Peṭ-Āḥāt, i. 51
Peṭhi, i. 211
Petra, ii. 36
Phallus of Neith, iii. 177
Pharaoh, ii. 32
Pharaohs, i. 188
Pierret, P., iii. 83
Pig of evil, ii. 161; iii. 160
Pits of fire, i. 249; iii. 143, 178, 179
Pleyte, Dr., iii. 84
Pool of Maāti, ii. 61
Powers, the Eight, ii. 230, 253; iii. 185
Ptaḥ, ii. 50
Ptaḥ Sekri, ii. 67
Pyramids of Gîza, iii. 10
Pyramid Texts, iii. 3, 12, 13

Qa-ha-ḥetep, iii. 39
Qaḥu, iii. 40

Qān, **ii.** 205; **iii.** 167
Qashefshef, **i.** 271
Qatā, **i.** 9
Qat-em-khu-s, **i.** 10
Qat-em-sepu-s, **i.** 266
Qa-Ṭemt, **ii.** 252
Qat-kheru-neheset-, etc., **iii.** 35
Qebḥsennuf, **i.** 135; **ii.** 273; **iii.** 188
Qema-ur, **iii.** 68
Qem-Ḥāp, **iii.** 83
Qenā, **ii.** 208, 209
Qenqenet, **iii.** 48
Qenqentet, **iii.** 64
Qeṭeṭ-Ṭent, **iii.** 137

RĀ, **ii.** 50, 82, 85, 91, 94, 98, 111, 116, 120, 126, 139, 140, 148, 154, 170, 180, 182, 194, 200, 205, 218, 224, 225, 230, 234, 243, 253, 257, 260, 265, 266, 271, 276, 280, 285, 288, 291, 297, 298; brotherhood of priests of, **iii.** 4; Forms of, **iii.** 192; Image of, **i.** 144; as Osiris, **iii.** 106; Soul of, **iii.** 169
Rā-Ḥeru-khuti, **i.** 267; **ii.** 140; **iii.** 38
Rā-khuti, **ii.** 130
Rameses VI., **iii.** 82
Rameses XII., **iii.** 21
Rams, the Four, **iii.** 154
Rations of the dead, **iii.** 170
Reapers, the Seven, **ii.** 178, 181
Red Crown, **i.** 208, 209, 216, 238, 297, 298
Red Crowns, **i.** 128, 134
Red Land, **ii.** 154
Re-en-qereret-àpt-khatu, **i.** 232, 233; **ii.** 36; **iii.** 99, 175
Regeneration, **iii.** 149
Rekem, **ii.** 61
Rekh, **i.** 240
Rekḥet-besu-ākhmet-, etc., **iii.** 34
Rekhit, **i.** 252
Relatives and their offerings, **iii.** 150
Remit, **i.** 53
Rem-neteru, **i.** 175
Reneniu, the, **ii.** 293, 297
Renen-sbau, **ii.** 274, 278
Renpeti, i. 33
Ren-thethen, **i.** 10
Rerek, **iii.** 39
Reri, **ii.** 301, 302, 304; **iii.** 102, 196
Rerit-ānkh, **i.** 183
Res-àb, **iii.** 31

Reset-åfu, i. 243
Re-sethau, ii. 14
Res-ḥrå, iii. 31
Re-statet, ii. 13
Re-stau, i. 62, 63, 73, 74; iii. 132, 134, 135
Resurrection, iii. 149
Reth = Egyptians, ii. 151, 153, 154; iii. 146
Rethenu, god of, ii. 274, 278
River of the Ṭuat, iii. 90
Rope, ii. 256, 257
Rubric, iii. 73
Ruti-Åsår, i. 140; ii. 25; iii. 151
Ruti-en-Åsår, iii. 98

Sa, i. 4, 140; ii. 82, 87, 91, 103, 120, 140, 191, 220, 240, 262, 282, 304, 305; iii. 109, 140
Saa-em-keb, i. 187; iii. 156
Sa-aḳeb, ii. 32; iii. 98
Saa-Set, ii. 86 ff.; iii. 100, 116
Sabes, iii. 31
Sa-em-ḳeb, iii. 98
Sāḥ, the god, ii. 217, 218
Sāḥ-åb, i. 52
Sailors of Rā, the Twelve, i. 188
Saïs, i. 238, 239; iii. 176, 177
Sait, i. 252; iii. 184
Sait, see Saïs
Sait, the, ii. 241
Saiu, the, ii. 241; iii. 184
Sar = Osiris, ii. 126, 161, 171, 178, 180, 189, 280; iii. 164; Circle of, i. 141
Sarthethaåth, i. 129
Satathenen, i. 153
Sati-ṭemui, iii. 38
Satiu, i. 102
Sau, ii. 280
Sba, Star-god, i. 41
Sbai, i. 11
Scales of Osiris, ii. 162, 164; iii. 159
Scarab, i. 134
Sceptres, gods of, ii. 292
Schack-Schackenburg, iii. 12
Schäfer, iii. 83
Scorpion, iii. 133
Scorpion Ānkhet, i. 73
Scythes, ii. 181
Seb, i. 136, 141, 172; ii. 51, 55, 170, 273, 283, 287, 305; iii. 67, 151, 163, 187; standards of, ii. 174, 183
Seb-qenbeti, i. 27

Sebȧ, i. 55; ii. 204, 205; iii. 124, 130
Sebȧ-Āpep, ii. 202, 206, 207
Sebȧ-Āpep-Ḥefau, iii. 167
Sebȧu, the, ii. 61
Sebaut-netchetet, ii. 289
Sebeḥu-f, i. 260
Sebekhti, ii. 284, 288; iii. 189
Sebek-Rā, ii. 89, 293
Seben-ḥesq-khaibitu, i. 29
Sebek-ḥrȧ, i. 179
Sebi, i. 214; ii. 301, 302, 304; iii. 102, 196
Sebit-nebt-uȧa-, etc., i. 233; ii. 36; iii. 99, 176
Sefȧ, i. 7
Seḥ, i. 57
Seḥert-baiu-s, i. 181-183; iii. 155
Seḥetch-ur, i. 4
Seḥith, i. 132
Sekem, the, iii. 171
Sekennu, i. 211
Seken-Ṭuatiu, i. 233
Seker, i. 86, 106; ii. 59; Āḥeth, chamber of, i. 81; body of, i. 65; iii. 132; chamber of, iii. 134, 135; Circle of, ii. 16; cult of, iii. 138; Image of, ii. 17; iii. 135, 139; Kingdom of, iii. 131, 134; Land of, ii. 13, 16; iii. 134-140; Ṭuat of, iii. 179
Sekhabesnefunen, ii. 100
Sekhem-ā-kheftiu, i. 29
Sekhemet-ṭesu-ḥent-, etc., iii. 32
Sekhem-ḥrȧ, i. 11
Sekhemiu, ii. 253; iii. 185
Sekhemu, ii. 230
Sekhen-khaibit, i. 166
Sekhennu, i. 234
Sekhen-Ṭuatiu, ii. 36; iii. 99
Sekhen-ur, iii. 35
Sekher-āṭ, iii. 39
Sekher-remus, iii. 39
Seker-shetau-ur-ā, i. 41
Sekhet, i. 4, 219; ii. 154, 155, 262; of Thebes, i. 30
Sekhet-Ȧanru, iii. 47
Sekhet-Ȧaru, ii. 63, 145, 150, 151, 217, 218; iii. 24, 27, 28, 198; pictures of, iii. 43-55; secret gates of, iii. 31, 37, 42, 49, 90; = Second Ȧat, iii. 38
Sekhet-em-kheftiu-s, i. 10
Sekhet-em-khu-s, i. 266
Sekhet-ḥetep (or Ḥetepet), ii. 63; iii. 38, 41, 44, 48,

49 ff., 64, 67, 85, 90, 138, 145, 198
Sekhet-ḥrȧ-āsht-ȧru, iii. 28
Sekhet-meṭu, i. 198
Sekhet-nebt-ḥetepet, ii. 217; iii. 168
Sekhit, i. 9
Sekhti, i. 8, 203
Seki, i. 11, 260
Sekmet-ḥer-ȧbt-uȧa-s, iii. 97
Sek-re, i. 7
Sekri, i. 93, 94, 116, 212; Eye of Horus, iii. 133; secret forms of, i. 98
Sekri-Utchat, i. 69
Sektet-Boat, i. 4, 6; iii. 105
Sem-ānkh, i. 70
Semetu, iii. 28
Sem-ḥer-ȧb-uȧa-s, ii. 17
Sem-Ḥeru, i. 222
Semi, ii. 263, 266; iii. 187
Semit-ḥer-ȧbt-uȧa-s, iii. 134
Sem-nebt-ḥet, i. 237, 238
Sem-Rā, i. 129, 130
Semsem, i. 234
Sem-shet, i. 237, 238
Semsu, ii. 25, 27; iii. 151
Sen, coffin of, iii. 55
Senket, i. 180
Senmekhef, i. 275; iii. 195
Senni gods, ii. 198, 199, 200
Sensȧbt, i. 267
Senṭ, ii. 170
Senthes, i. 230
Sent-nef-Amentiu, i. 109
Sepa, iii. 68, 69, 70
Sepāshāt, i. 57
Sepṭ, ii. 288, 291
Sepṭat-ānkh, i. 185
Septet-uauau, ii. 102; iii. 100, 125
Sepṭ-metu, ii. 20; iii. 97, 148
Sepulchres, the Nine, iii. 140
Seqenen-Rā III., iii. 16, 17
Seqer-ṭepu, i. 156
Seqet-ḥra, iii. 31
Ser, iii. 151, 154
Sereq, ii. 262
Serpent boat, iii. 133
Serq, } i. 141, 143; iii.
Serqet, } 152, 188
Serser, Lake of, ii. 227-231; iii. 170
Sert-nehepu-em-, etc., iii. 36
Sesent-khu, i. 30
Sesheta, i. 170; iii. 153
Sesheta-baiu, i. 166
Seshet-māket-neb-s, iii. 96
Seshsesh, iii. 183
Seshshȧ, ii. 274, 278

Sessi, ii. 241, 244; iii. 183, 185
Set, i. 29; ii. 47, 248, 299; iii. 189; god of funeral mountain, ii. 80; iii. 100, 109; bull-headed, i. 109; the Everlasting, i. 249; the Watcher, iii. 174
Set-Åmentet, iii. 100, 110
Seṭa-ta, ii. 119
Setchet, ii. 88
Seṭefiu, the Four, ii. 272; iii. 188
Set-em-ḥrà-f, i. 47
Set-em-maat-f, i. 49; ii. 159, 168, 169; iii. 101, 158
Seṭfit, ii. 175, 218
Seth-àb, i. 147
Seth-ḥeḥ, i. 255; iii. 177
Sethen-ḥāt, i. 69
Set-Horus, ii. 247, 251, 263, 267
Set-ḥrà, ii. 219, 220, 221; iii. 101, 169
Sethu, ii. 259-261; iii. 101, 187
Seti I., i. 166; ii. 46, 50-69, 161; iii. 23, 26, 82, 84, 89; alabaster sarcophagus of, ii. 43 ff.
Seti, the serpent, ii. 108, 111
Set-nehes, i. 231
Seṭti, ii. 292
Setu, i. 211
Seuatchet-àtebui-pet, i. 265
Sharpe, S., ii. 45, 46; iii. 83
Shatheth, i. 78
Shef-ḥrà, ii. 171
Shefshef, i. 48
Sheftu, i. 10
Shēkh-Abâda, iii. 11
Shemat-khu, i. 197
Shemerti, i. 209, 211
Shemsu, i. 260; iii. 154
Shemti, ii. 248, 249, 252; iii. 186
Shenit, i. 14
Shennu beings, ii. 52, 111
Shen-ten-Åmm, i. 200
Sheol, iii. 88
Shepes, i. 147
Shepherd Kings, iii. 16
Shepi, ii. 190
Shepu, i. 236
Shesat-māket-neb-s, ii. 5; iii. 111
Sheserà, i. 210
Sheseṭ-ḳerḥ-mātet-neb-s, i. 12
Shesshes, ii. 241, 242
Sheta-àb, ii. 158
Shetai, i. 66

Shetat-besu, ii. 279-281; iii. 102, 188
Sheṭāu, ii. 279
Sheṭu, i. 234, 242; iii. 177
Shrines, the Twelve, iii. 128
Shu, i. 4, 98, 136; ii. 51, 170, 305; iii. 71, 89, 151, 193; Image of, i. 171, 278
Sinai, i. 270; iii. 146, 194
Sky-goddess, iii. 24
Sleepers in Osiris, iii. 167
Sma-kheftiu-f, i. 51
Smau, a lake, iii. 49
Smamti, iii. 34
Soane, Sir John, ii. 43
Sothis, iii. 42, 113
Soul-goddesses, i. 20
Soul of double Bull, ii. 106
Soul of Rā, ii. 107, 258
Soul, the Great, i. 9; iii. 107
Souls, destroyers of, iii. 42
Souls of Ȧment, ii. 253, 255; iii. 185
Souls of Serser, ii. 228
Souls of Ṭuat, i. 1
Souls, secret, i. 1
Souls, the Nine, iii. 169, 170
South, gods of, ii. 245, 246, 252
South, Kings of, ii. 293, 296
South, Queens of, ii. 294, 298
Spearmen, ii. 242
Spert-neter-s, i. 262
Sphinxes, the Two, iii. 135
Spirits of the East, ii. 292
Spirits, seat of, iii. 47
Sta-en-Ȧsȧr-, etc., iii. 36
Standards of Sar, Seb, Set, Shu, Horus, Kheperȧ, Rā, ii. 170, 173, 183; iii. 189
Star-gods, ii. 263, 266
Stat, i. 201
Stau, iii. 119
Strabo, iii. 21
Stream of Osiris, etc., ii. 9, 20
Submerged, the, i. 224
Sûdân, iii. 17, 146
Sulphur springs, iii. 129
Sunrise, Mount of, iii. 150, 173, 176
Suten-ḥenen, iii. 5
Suteniu, i. 118; iii. 148
Swimmers, i. 224; ii. 223; iii. 169

TA, i. 179
Tait, i. 158
Takhāau, iii. 83
Tanen, ii. 132, 161
Ṭat, ii. 80
Tat, iii. 100, 109
Ta-tchesert, i. 40; ii. 65

Ta-thenen, i. 136, 138, 166; ii. 230; iii. 151; Images of, i. 168, 169; iii. 154, 155; soul of, i. 171
Ṭaṭṭu (Mendes), iii. 65
Tatubȧ, ii. 5; iii. 115
Tchamuti, i. 203
Tchatcha, Tchatchau, i. 188, 197; ii. 32; iii. 129, 130, 147, 157, 169; of the Ṭuat, ii. 151; who repulse Āpep, ii. 113
Tchaṭiu, the Four, iii. 188
Tchat-Ṭuat, i. 11, 190
Tchatui, i. 8
Tchau, i. 142; iii. 152
Tchaunnut, i. 5
Tchebā, i. 20
Tcheb-neter, i. 50
Tchefet, iii. 48
Tcheḥrȧ, ii. 161
Tcheḥtcheḥ, i. 9
Tcher-khu, i. 182
Tchesef, iii. 35
Tcheserit, iii. 101, 186
Tchesert, Gate, ii. 259; iii. 8, 10
Tchesert, Lake, iii. 49
Tcheṭbi, ii. 120; iii. 100, 140
Tcheṭ-ḥrȧ, iii. 83
Tcheṭmit, i. 230
Tchets, i. 242
Tears of Rā, iii. 146
Ṭeba, i. 53, 194
Ṭebai, i. 271
Ṭebat, i. 181
Ṭebat-neteru-s, i. 161; iii. 98, 154
Ṭebat-neteru-set, ii. 30
Ṭeb-ḥer-kehaat, iii. 31
Ṭebi-neter, i. 50
Tefnet, i. 15, 172; ii. 57; iii. 71
Teḥuti-ḥer-khent-f, i. 28
Teḥuti-khenti-neb-Ṭuat, i. 117
Teka-ḥrȧ, i. 46; ii. 139, 140; iii. 101, 143
Tekait, i. 200
Tekmi, ii. 139
Tell al-ʻAmarna, ii. 43
Tem, i. 136; ii. 96, 113, 116, 117, 170, 301; iii. 67; Image of, i. 144, 171
Temau, i. 210
Tem-sia-er-, etc., iii. 36
Ṭemṭet, i. 181
Ṭemṭith, i. 143
Ṭemṭu, i. 194
Ṭemu, iii. 129, 130, 135, 151, 177, 179
Ṭenit, i. 143
Ṭens-sma-kekiu, i. 176

Ṭent, ii. 288, 291
Ṭent-baiu, i. 50; iii. 97, 121
Ṭenṭenit, i. 11
Ṭenṭenit - ḥesq (uḥeset) - khak-ȧb, i. 208; ii. 34; iii. 99, 172
Ṭep, City of, ii. 61
Ṭepȧn, i. 97, 98; iii. 136
Ṭepḥet-sheta, ii. 25; iii. 98
Ṭepi, i. 190; ii. 248, 251, 252; iii. 186
Ṭept-bes-s, i. 57
Ṭept-ḥrȧ, i. 210
Ṭepu, i. 31
Ṭepui, i. 243
Ṭeri, ii. 218
Terms, the Four, i. 4
Ṭert-neshen, i. 200
Ṭes-āḥā-Tathenen, i. 171
Ṭes-ākhem-baiu, i. 173
Ṭes-amem-mit-em-sheta-f, i. 185; iii. 155
Ṭesem-ḥrȧ-f, i. 47
Ṭeser-ā, i. 155
Ṭeser-ȧbt, i. 262
Ṭeser-ȧri, i. 206
Ṭesert-ȧnt, i. 197
Ṭesert-baiu, Gate, ii. 130, 252, 301, 302; iii. 102, 141, 195, 196
Ṭes-khaibitu-Ṭuatiu, i. 177; iii. 155
Ṭes-khu, i. 183, 272
Ṭes-neb-terer-. . . ., i. 170
Ṭes-Rā-kheftiu-f, i. 179
Ṭes-sekhem-ȧru, i. 180
Ṭes-sepṭ-nesut, i. 181
Ṭes-sheta-theḥen-neteru, i. 174
Ṭeshet-ṭesheru, iii. 12
Ṭeṭ, house of, i. 59
Tetȧ, iii. 3
Ṭeṭet, iii. 69
Ṭet-sem-ermen, i. 177
Ṭeṭu, iii. 69
Thath-neteru, i. 129
Thebaïd, iii. 5
Thebes, ii. 43; iii. 5, 15, 16, 41, 51, 149; Anubis of, i. 51
Theḥbith, i. 125
Thema, i. 53
Thema-re, i. 273
Themath-erment, i. 220
Themeḥu, ii. 151, 153, 155; iii. 146
Thenȧ, i. 260
Then-en-neteru, ii. 38
Then-neteru, i. 256 ff.; iii. 100, 191
Thenṭ-ent-baiu, ii. 10
Thepḥet-Ȧsȧr, i. 139
Thepḥet-Sheta, i. 140; iii. 151

Thes-ḥrȧu, son of Sekri, **i.** 208, 212; **iii.** 173
Thest-ȧpt, **i.** 78
Thes-ṭepu-neteru, **i.** 269
Thesu, **i.** 211
Thet-em-ḳerḥ, **i.** 53
Thettu, **i.** 50
Thoth, **i.** 69, 116; **ii.** 69, 163, 253, 255; **iii.** 50, 51, 159, 160
Thoth and Horus, **iii.** 133
Thoth and Utchat, **i.** 82
Thothmes I., **iii.** 21
Thothmes III., **iii.** 8, 23
Tiāmat, **iii.** 184
Time in Ȧmentet, **ii.** 151
Tombs at Thebes, **iii.** 21
Tortoise, **ii.** 51, 52
Truth, **ii.** 95
Ṭ-semu-em-maat-f, **i.** 156
Ṭ-semu-nes-f, **i.** 155
Ṭua-Ḥeru, **i.** 243
Ṭuai, **i.** 13
Ṭuamutef, **i.** 135; **ii.** 50, 273; **iii.** 188
Ṭuat, Antechamber of, **ii.** 80; Bark of, **ii.** 106, 107; Circle of, **i.** 171-173; **iii.** 155; Divisions of, **iii.** 93; meaning of name, **iii.** 87; = Osiris, **ii.** 306; Souls of, **i.** 1
Ṭuats, the Four, **iii.** 179-181
Ṭuatet-māketet-en-neb-s, **i.** 187; **iii.** 99, 156
Ṭuatheth, **i.** 157
Ṭuati, **i.** 14, 154, 272; **ii.** 200, 210, 216, 287; **iii.** 167
Ṭuatiu, **i.** 56
Tui (?), **ii.** 230
Ṭui-qam-āāiu, **iii.** 38
Ṭun-en-maā, **i.** 66
Tun-ḥāt, **iii.** 31
Two Faces, god of, **i.** 29; **ii.** 267

UA-ȦB, **i.** 268
Uȧa-herer, **i.** 46
Uȧa-penāt, **i.** 45
Uȧa-ta, **iii.** 126
Uȧat-ṭesṭes, **i.** 158
Uāau, **iii.** 31
Uakh, **iii.** 48
Uamemti, **ii.** 272, 273
Uart-ent-mu, **iii.** 41
Uatch-ḥrȧ, **i.** 69
Unȧs, **iii.** 3
Underworld, **iii.** 88
Unen-em-ḥetep, **iii.** 48
Unnut-sethaiut, **ii.** 273
Unt, **iii.** 40
Unta, **i.** 9

Unti, ii. 262, 265; iii. 187; Circle of, ii. 276
Uraei, fiery, iii. 157
Uraei, Lake of living, ii. 127, 131; iii. 141
Uraei, the divine, ii. 259
Ur-ḥekau, i. 52
Ur-ḳert, i. 154
Urnes, i. 6, 19, 20, 21, 24, 36, 40; ii. 4; iii. 96, 105, 111, 112, 116
Urṭ, i. 135
Urt-ȧmt-Ṭuat, i. 11
Urt-em-sekhemu-set, ii. 14; iii. 97, 132
Uru gods, i. 41
Usert, Lake, iii. 49
Ushemet-ḥatu-kheftiu-Rā, i. 20; ii. 2; iii. 96
Ushem-ḥāt-kheftiu-s, i. 12
Usrit, i. 219
Utau gods, ii. 107
Utcha, ii. 274, 278
Utchat, i. 69, 82
Utchats, the, ii. 170
Uthesu, i. 69
Ut-meṭ, i. 70
Ut-meṭu, i. 86
Ut-meṭu-Ȧsȧr, i. 5
Ut-meṭu-Kheperȧ, i. 5
Ut-meṭu-Rā, i. 4
Ut-meṭu-Tem, i. 5
Uṭu, i. 210

Valley of Ṭuat, ii. 47
Valley of Kings' Tombs, ii. 43
Venus, i. 115

Wâdî Ḥammâmât, iii. 7
Water of Ta-thenen, i. 138
Weaving instruments, iii. 157
Weepers, the, ii. 293, 296
Wheat in Ṭuat, iii. 41
Wheat-god, ii. 180; gods, iii. 164
White Crown, i. 208, 209, 216, 238; ii. 280, 297, 298; crowns, i. 128
Wiedemann, Prof. A., iii. 164
Wigs, ii. 200
Winds, goddesses of, i. 265
Womb of Nut, iii. 197
Worm, the, ii. 245

Yâḳûṭ, iii. 89

Xoïs, iii. 16

GILBERT AND RIVINGTON LTD., ST. JOHN'S HOUSE, CLERKENWELL, E.C.

www.ingramcontent.com/pod-product-compliance
Lightning Source LLC
Chambersburg PA
CBHW040250170426
43191CB00018B/2361
* 9 7 8 1 6 3 1 8 2 8 3 3 1 *